S0-CFS-715

Betty Smith has once again reached into her store of life experiences, and her knowledge and love of scripture, to bring us a hearty banquet of *soul food*! Her insights into how God works in lives and situations, along with her down-to-earth understanding of the relationship between us and our Maker speaks of her own relationship with Him. She's also quite adept at turning a thought into a poem. Maybe her next book will be all verse, but I doubt it; she loves the poetry of the Bible too much. So glad to call her my friend, and so lucky to be blessed by her teaching every week!

—LINDA CRUSSELLE, VICE PRESIDENT
THE CRUSSELLE COMPANY, REGISTERED LAND SURVEYORS

A book entitled *Taters and Peas* is as enticing as knowing the author of such a book. Being a lover of cooking and eating, it is easy to be taught by the analogies of Betty's stories. Some of the best lessons are learned in the kitchen and around the dinner table. We can all relate to the satisfaction of our taste buds being happy and our belly being full. Likewise, we know the disappointment of something tasting bad and the growl of being hungry.

This book encourages us to be the delicious people we were created to be and also not to display characteristics that are bitter and tasteless. At one point, she says we must be Jesus with skin on to all those we meet—what a sweet flavor to pass on to others!

Betty is a great communicator of God's Word through her stories and poetry. It is a treat to be able to learn under Betty, because her teachings are not just her opinions but are backed up by scripture—our Creator's words. She shares from the heart her mistakes and temptations to inspire us that, as we go through the valleys, there is victory in being faithful and steadfast in His promises.

This book will remain close by so that I can pull it out to remind me of the life God intended for each one of us.

—June Rainwater, Youth Director
Powder Springs First United Methodist Church,
Powder Springs, GA

This is an amazing compilation of scriptures and their applications to life.

—Betty Vollenweider
Ahni & Zoe by Creative Memories Consultant

As with her previous books, Betty Smith's latest effort, *Taters and Peas*, is infused with her love for God and her zeal for glorifying Him in her writing. She writes the way she talks; and the way she uses words reflects the way she lives her life, with faith and enthusiasm.

From the very beginning, would-be readers are intrigued by the provocative title, *Taters and Peas*. What kind of book is this? Is it a cookbook? If it is, how has the author given spiritual significance to the recipes? Well, you might say it is similar to a cookbook, but in *Taters and Peas* the author has skillfully mixed format and content to create a delightful concoction that feeds not the physical body, but the soul and spirit.

The heading for each chapter uses either a "tater" or a "pea." The "tater" chapters are given titles such as "Partici-pi-Tator" or "Spec-Tator." The "Peas" chapters are entitled with words beginning with the letter "P." The captivating chapter titles have an aura of mystery as to what their content could be. Each one, chapter after chapter, invites the inquisitive reader to come inside and share what the author has cooked up to reflect its particular title.

Betty Smith's own life has been very eventful. She has traveled over the world and in this country, participating in mission trips and lay witness efforts. Her life's journey has been booby trapped by unexpected negative events, as well as joyful ones. Writing with transparency and journalistic expertise, she gives readers glimpses into her life and family—the ups, the downs, the grief, and the triumphs—all the time drawing them with her into the circle of God's faithfulness. The written words tell how her own faith and trust in the love, power, and protection of the Lord Jesus Christ has given her victory over everything that has come against her, encouraging readers to aspire to that same kind of faith in their own lives.

Layered within the narrative are generous portions of inspiring and well chosen scriptures. The combination of narrative and appropriate scriptures alone makes this book so worth the reading, but there is more. Each chapter is topped off with a poem! The poems are original creations of the author and are suited to the content of that particular chapter.

All in all, *Taters and Peas* is like one extended devotional treat. There are multiple chapters, but when readers complete the last one, they will find themselves wishing for another helping. I heartily recommend this book for a unique inspirational experience.
—MARY KIRKLAND KNIGHT
RETIRED LABORATORY AND
QUALITY ASSURANCE PROFESSIONAL,
INDEPENDENT WRITER/EDITOR,
DALLAS, GA

What kind of "Tater" are you? Are you a "spec-tater"? Or, are you a "participa-tater"? Are you an "immi-tater"? Or, are you an "irri-tater"? Do you cheer others on or do you run the race? Do you do great things or do you add to the applause? When you first read this book you may think it

simple but when you make self comparisons it takes on new
meanings. Read it twice

—Tom Williams<br>President, Quality Development Company,<br>Lieutenant Colonel USAF (retired)

# BETTY TERRY SMITH

CREATION
HOUSE

Taters and Peas: How God Uses "P's" (Promises, Prayer, Protection, Perseverance and Praise) to Produce "Sweet Taters" by Betty Terry Smith
A Charisma Media Company
600 Rinehart Road
Lake Mary, Florida 32746
www.charismamedia.com

This book or parts thereof may not be reproduced in any form, stored in a retrieval system, or transmitted in any form by any means—electronic, mechanical, photocopy, recording, or otherwise—without prior written permission of the publisher, except as provided by United States of America copyright law.

Unless otherwise noted, all Scripture quotations are from the New King James Version of the Bible. Copyright © 1979, 1980, 1982 by Thomas Nelson, Inc., publishers. Used by permission.

Scripture quotations marked KJV are from the King James Version of the Bible.

Scripture quotations marked THE MESSAGE are from *The Message: The Bible in Contemporary English*, copyright © 1993, 1994, 1995, 1996, 2000, 2001, 2002. Used by permission of NavPress Publishing Group.

Scripture quotations marked NIV are from the Holy Bible, New International Version. Copyright © 1973, 1978, 1984, 2010, 2011, International Bible Society. Used by permission.

Scripture quotations marked TLB are from The Living Bible. Copyright © 1971. Used by permission of Tyndale House Publishers, Inc., Wheaton, IL 60189. All rights reserved.

Unless otherwise noted, all English definitions are from *Webster's New American Dictionary*, New York: Books, 1968.

Greek and Hebrew definitions are from James Strong, *Strong's Exhaustive Concordance of the Bible*, McLean, VA: MacDonald Publishing, ISBN 0-917006-01-1.

Unless otherwise noted, all poems are the author's original.

Design Director: Bill Johnson
Cover design by Judy McKittrick Wright

Copyright © 2014 by Betty Smith
All rights reserved.

Visit the author's website: www.bettyterrysmith.com.

Library of Congress CataloginginPublication Data: 2014937540
International Standard Book Number: 978-1-62136-748-2
E-book International Standard Book Number:
978-1-62136-749-9

While the author has made every effort to provide accurate
telephone numbers and Internet addresses at the time of
publication, neither the publisher nor the author assumes
any responsibility for errors or for changes that occur after
publication.

First edition

14 15 16 17 18 — 987654321
Printed in Canada

*In loving memory of Muther and Daddy,*
*the best cheerleaders a girl ever had!*

# CONTENTS

# ACKNOWLEDGMENTS

THIS IS A great big thank you to all my families:

First, my immediate family of precious jewels, who are my most enthusiastic fans and who add "life" to my life. The only way I could be prouder of you would be if there were two of me!

Second, my "family of God" at Powder Springs First United Methodist Church. In you I find encouragement, edification and exhortation. Your faith multiplies my faith and I am enriched.

Third, all the "families of God," who have invited me to come and speak, received me warmly as one of their own, and shared with me their stories. I have seen a preview of heaven, where all the saints will be gathered together.

Last, but not my any means least, my family at Charisma Media/Creation House. I appreciate your talents and unique gifts as you have worked as a team to present my fourth book to the public, with the common goal of making disciples—moving people closer to God.

The Lord has done awesome things for me through my families—and I am so glad!

# Introduction

**H**AVE YOU EVER attended church and found that you were more impacted by the children's sermonette than by the sermon itself? That happened to me once; and I find that the more I dwell on it, the deeper it gets into my spirit and the more facets of truth I see.

The teacher gathered the children around her in a semi-circle. Of course, the children were delightful and the congregation was blessed before a word was spoken. The teacher sweetly smiled at each one; and then from a bag she held, she gently removed a white potato (in the South you might say a "tater"). She called it a "common-tater," and made some brief comments about how special the children were, definitely not common. Next she removed another tater. It had "eyes," which made it a "spec-tater." They were encouraged to get into the game, not just watch. Another tater was an "irri-tater." Of course, children don't want to irritate their moms and dads, teachers, and those in authority. The "imi-tater" came next and the children were cautioned to choose carefully those they want to imitate. The last tater was the "sweet tater," and the children were exhorted to make this their goal because everyone, especially Jesus, loves sweet taters. The congregation clapped as the children, these sweet taters, were dismissed to join their families.

Thus these words were planted in my heart, and they began to grow, like taters in good dirt. In the Parable of the Sower (Mark 4:20), Jesus said:

But these are the ones sown on good ground, those who hear the word, accept it, and bear fruit: some thirtyfold, some sixty, and some a hundred.

As I examined each tater, meditated, and pondered, I saw new light—how each one held a life lesson. However, along with the taters, I recognized some "P's," (peas), such as promises, prayer, protection, perseverance, praise, and promotion.

Dear Reader, I invite you to dine with me on some taters and peas.

# Chapter 1
# Common-Tater

**W**E CAN APPROACH "common taters" in two different ways. First, as being common, ordinary, and not special; it can even mean inferior or low class. Secondly, we can make a play on words and use "comment-taters" (commentators). That would mean a person who gives a commentary or an analysis. This is especially used for reporters on radio and television who comment on the news of the day or who appear at the conclusion of another person's speech or interview to tell the public what the speaker really meant—assuming that the common public cannot grasp the truth for itself.

In Acts 10 there is an account of Peter being summoned to the house of Cornelius, a Gentile. The Lord prepared Peter for this assignment through a vision. He had gone up on the housetop to pray around noon, and he was very hungry. He fell into a trance and saw heaven open and a great sheet bound at the four corners that was let down to earth and appeared before him. On the sheet were all kinds of four-footed animals, wild beasts, creeping things, and birds. A voice told Peter to kill and eat, but Peter protested. In verses 14–15 we read:

> "Not so, Lord! For I have never eaten anything *common* or unclean." And a voice spoke to him again the

second time, "What God has cleansed you must not call *common.*"
                                    —ACTS 10:14–15, EMPHASIS ADDED

Peter obeys the Lord, and goes to meet Cornelius, as well as Cornelius' relatives and close friends. Peter makes an interesting comment in verse 28:

> You know how unlawful it is for a Jewish man to keep company with or go to one of another nation. But God has shown me that I should not call any man *common* or unclean.
>                                    —ACTS 10:28, EMPHASIS ADDED

Peter then preached the peace of Jesus Christ, the Lord of all—how God had anointed Jesus of Nazareth with the Holy Spirit and with power and how Jesus went about doing good and healing all who were oppressed by the devil. He went further to explain the crucifixion and the resurrection. While he was speaking, the Holy Spirit fell upon all who heard his words. Peter and his Jewish companions were astonished that the Holy Spirit had been poured out on the Gentiles (vv. 36–48).

Joel had prophesied in Joel 2:28: "And it shall come to pass afterward That I will pour out My Spirit on all flesh."

In the Living Bible we see the value of a human being in Psalm 49:9:

> For a soul is far too precious to be ransomed by mere earthly wealth. There is not enough of it in all the earth to buy eternal life for just one soul, to keep it out of hell.

It took the precious, spotless blood of the Son of God to pay our ransom, to release us from that debt of sin that we owed but could never pay. He shed that blood seven times, the number of perfection. First was in the Garden of Gethsemane, where He sweat drops of blood (Luke 22:44); His disciples fell asleep and did not pray with Him. Second was before the Sanhedrin, where the religious leaders had Him beaten (Luke 22:63)—He was treated with contempt by the temporary high priest, yet He was the eternal High Priest (Mark 14:63–65). Third was before Pilate, where He was scourged (John 19:1). Fourth, also before Pilate, He bled when a crown of thorns was placed on His head (v. 2). Fifth was when the soldiers nailed the hands of Jesus and, sixth, the feet of Jesus to the cross (John 20:25, 27; Ps. 22:16). And finally, seventh, was when the soldier pierced His side with a spear and water and blood poured out (John 19:34).

John 3:16 is further evidence that the Father considers all the human race to be special, extraordinary—so much so that He planned for their eternal security:

> For God so loved the world that He gave His only begotten Son, that *whosoever* believes in Him should not perish but have everlasting life.
> —JOHN 3:16, EMPHASIS ADDED

Everybody is a "whosoever." Not a single, solitary person on the face of this earth is common or inferior; and each and every one has been given the option of eternal life through the sacrifice of Jesus, the Son of God. It is a gift given at great expense. However, a gift must be received.

David was my dear friend; he was married to Laura. He had attended law school with my husband Bob. Our first-born son, Steve, was born in April 1959 and their firstborn daughter, Denise, followed in December. Later Bob and I had another son and a daughter while David and Laura had two more sons. We went on family vacations together and met regularly for Saturday night suppers and to play cards. Sad to say, David and Laura divorced and later Bob and I did the same, leaving broken hearts along the way.

These were strange divorces in that we still loved our mates. David had remarried and moved to Missouri, where subsequently his wife died, leaving him very bitter. His health began to decline so he moved home to Georgia. Bob had divorced his second wife and moved to Mississippi; then he, too, had returned to Georgia. Bob and I were to visit David one particular weekend, but he begged off, saying he was not feeling well.

David and I had a conversation on the phone, and he admitted he was angry at God for taking his wife. We talked a very long time as I tried to get him to forgive God and himself, to accept this gift of love from the Father, and to call on the name of Jesus. Then he said, "You almost have me persuaded," reminding me of the time Paul heard those words from King Agrippa (Acts 26:28). David said goodbye and we never had another conversation; he died a few days later.

I wrote the following poem in memory of my friend:

## By Way of the Cross

My friend died suddenly today and there is sadness
    in my heart.
There was more I had to say to him before we had to
    part.
I had more evidence with which to build my case,
But he left me with tears running down my face.

I tried before to tell him, but he just wouldn't listen,
Still I was sure I had more time to complete my
     mission.
He just had to know before he left this earth
That Jesus died for him because he had such worth!

The cross is the bridge reaching from earth to
     heaven,
There is only One Way—not four or five, or six or
     seven.
The cry of our Lord's heart is that none would be
     lost;
That all would come home by way of the Cross.

I pray that my friend is with Jesus and the angels in
     glory,
Learning with excitement and joy the truth of God's
     story.
We are the reason for the crucifixion and
     resurrection—
Jesus provided Himself as the Great Connection.

It's so hard, being left with this big question mark.
Did my friend make it to heaven, or did he not?
My soul rests in the unfailing love of my Lord.
Jesus did all He could—how can we ask for more?

I'm trusting in my Lord and in His goodness today,
That somehow He came in time and showed him the
     Way;
That my friend gladly took the Master by the hand,
And was ushered into heaven's Promised Land.

   In today's world we are known more by a number than by
our name. We have Social Security numbers, telephone and
cell numbers, insurance policy numbers, driver's license

numbers, account numbers, and PIN (personal identification) numbers. Our cars are registered with VIN numbers, and even our homes are numbered. Avis Car Rentals has turned this number system into a clever advertising slogan: "We Are Number Two So We Try Harder!"

Our world is impersonal; however, our God is very personal. He knows the number of hairs on our head (you have to be very close for that), and He keeps our tears in a bottle (Matt. 10:30; Ps. 56:8). His thoughts turn to us many times in a day, even more than the grains of sand on the seashore (Ps. 139:17–18). He knows where we are at all times. We can be on the top of the highest mountain or in the depths of the sea; but even there, He finds us (vv. 8–9). Nothing can separate us from His love—"neither death nor life, nor angels nor principalities nor powers, nor things present nor things to come, nor height nor depth, nor any other created thing" (Rom. 8:38–39).

Did you ever write your sweetheart's name in the palm of your hand, and draw a heart around it? Jesus has your name in the palm of His hand (Isa. 49:16). He says, "I have called you by your name; You are Mine" (43:1). We are His beloved (Rom. 11:28).

God even selected our parents, our families, our boundaries (Ps. 139:13–16; Acts 17:26), and He calls us His "offspring" (Acts 17:28). Of course, He hears His children when they pray (1 John 5:14–15). Jesus gave us a prayer guide, the Lord's Prayer (Luke 11:1–4); and when we just don't know how to pray, the Holy Spirit helps us (Rom. 8:26).

The most amazing thing is that He chose us! Jesus said, "You did not choose Me, but I chose you and appointed you that you should go and bear fruit" (John 15:16). It gets better: "For we are His workmanship, created in Christ

Jesus for good works, which God prepared beforehand that we should walk in them" (Eph. 2:10).

Is this not amazing love—the greatest good news! The Father has given us eternal life, and this life is in His Son, our Lord Jesus Christ. It is His gift (Rom. 6:23). He has blessed us with the greatest gift of all, and we want to bless Him in return. How can we, in these frail earth suits, bless the Supreme Blesser? Answer: by presenting our bodies back to Him, as our reasonable service (Rom. 12:1); and by reaching out to the least of His, spreading His love to everyone (Matt. 25:40).

As Christians (Christ-Ones), we have our marching orders. Jesus said: "Go therefore and make disciples" (Matt. 28:19). That means to move someone closer to God. We proceed with the blessed assurance that we personally matter to God; therefore, we may boldly approach our Father's throne of grace (Heb. 4:16). The Holy Spirit empowers us (Acts 1:8), and angels minister unto us (Heb. 1:14).

I was scheduled to be the main speaker at a women's retreat, and I wanted to open with the illustration of "taters." My problem was that I had only two taters, one regular white and one with eyes, so on my way I went into a supermarket to purchase a sweet tater. I was in the express lane so I could be on my way without delay.

There was one woman ahead of me and she was purchasing cigarettes; therefore, the clerk had to leave her register and go to the locked case that held the tobacco products. The customer turned to me, saying she was sorry for the delay. I assured her that there was no problem, but I was sorry she smoked because it wasn't good for her body. She said she had tried to stop many times but just could not, so I asked if we would pray about it. She completed her purchase, I paid for my sweet tater, and we stepped over to a quieter corner. She had not been attending church even though she was a believer in Christ, so I encouraged her to get back into fellowship so she could hear the Word and build her faith. Then we held hands and I prayed for her freedom from the bondage to the addiction to cigarettes. She was "happy" crying and we hugged goodbye. Because God loved her so much and she mattered to Him, He arranged this divine appointment. He wanted His daughter to be free and back in fellowship, and He used me as His instrument. What an honor!

Planet Earth is filled with other people who also matter to God, but many do not know they are loved. We must spread the good news because time is short. We cannot take *things* with us when we go to heaven, but we can take *people*. Let's get up loads—to the glory of our Father, in the name of Jesus, by the power of the Holy Spirit. We can bring a smile to the face of God merely by our "reasonable service."

You have heard it said, "God didn't make any junk!" Well, God didn't make any common taters either. In fact, there's not a "common" one in the whole bunch, and that brings a smile to our face.

While at the cemetery to put flowers on my parents' graves, I observed their headstones with their names and dates of birth and death. I was meditating on their lives, from their births to the year of my birth, and realized I did not know much about them up to then. I thought about what they had accomplished during just my lifetime. Then I wondered about me, what would be on my tombstone, so I wrote the following poem. I give you permission to insert your name instead of mine.

# BETTY TERRY SMITH: 1934–20___

To be born is an important thing,
For to finish, you must begin.
But it's what happens in the "dash" that counts—
That meaty part between the start and the end.

You have no control over your beginning.
God gave you life at His whim,
But what you do with the middle—
That's up to you: Your gift to Him.

On "that day" you will stand before His judgment
    seat,
To give an accounting of what you did with your
    "dash."
Did you increase or diminish His kingdom?
Did you leave His earth better or worse?

Oh, child of God, He gave you a beginning and an
    expected end.
Fill up the dash with those things that count for
    eternity,
That bring a smile to the face of God.

## Chapter 2
# COMMENT-TATER

THEN THERE ARE the "comment-taters" (commenta-tors). We were created with two ears and one mouth, so it stands to reason that we should listen twice as much as we talk. But it seems the reverse is true; we talk more than twice as much as we listen. And it is common knowledge that women talk much more than men. Watch the next time you are in a group. Husbands stand and smile and nod, while their wives let their words flow like foun-tains. That's just the way it is—the nature of the beast. (I know because I am one—a woman, that is, hopefully not a beast.)

My friend was going through a very difficult time and I was trying to encourage her, speaking cheerful words. When she had enough of this Pollyanna attitude, she quoted to me Proverbs 25:20: "Like one who takes away a garment in cold weather, and like vinegar on soda, is one who sings songs to a heavy heart."

My friend needed a listening ear, not a running mouth. I needed to let her talk, for "He who answers a matter before he hears it, It is folly and shame to him" (Prov. 18:13). King Solomon says, "To everything there is a season, a time for every purpose under heaven…a time to keep silence, and a time to speak" (Eccl. 3:1, 7). Oh, for the gift of knowing what time it is!

We also tend to believe what is printed in newspapers

and magazines, and especially what is spoken on radio and television by the so-called experts. Hitler's method of operation was to shout the lie time after time after time, and eventually the people came to believe what he said. And there is the Internet—it must be true if it's on the Internet! There is an amusing commercial in which a pretty young girl is questioned by a young man as to why she believes she has a date with a rich and handsome Frenchman as the result of a dating service. Her reply, "It's on the Internet!" As they are speaking, a rather plain big man with a scraggly beard, dressed in jeans and a baggy sweatshirt, and wearing a beret tilted to one side, comes to her side, saying, "Bon Jour," in a drawling Southern accent. So much for the validity of the Internet!

How do we know what is truth? Approximately 2,000 years ago Pilate asked Jesus that same question. Upon His arrest, Jesus told Pilate that He had come to bear witness to the truth. He said, "'Everyone who is of the truth hears My voice.' Pilate said to Him, 'What is truth?'" (John 18:37–38). Pilate immediately walks away, not wanting to know the truth, because for him the cost would be more than he was willing to pay. The day would come, however, when Pilate would come face to face with a resurrected Jesus Christ, the truth and the way and the life (John 14:6).

Eternal life is described in John 17:3 as knowing (having relationship with, as a man "knows" his wife) the only true God (the Father), and Jesus Christ whom He has sent. Jesus is our "way," and He is the only way, because no one comes to the Father except through Him (14:6). What a shame that Pilate did not seize this golden opportunity to "know" Jesus.

As members of this human race, we will be constantly tested to know what is truth; or perhaps it would be more correct to say, "*Who* is truth." Fortunately for us, this is an open book test. Our Lord wrote down all the answers in His Book, the BIBLE (Basic Instructions Before Leaving Earth). Here we find what God has to say about everything we will come to face in this life.

Many say they cannot understand the Bible, but we can just live by the parts we do understand and then mature into the rest. The Holy Spirit promised to be our Helper, teach us all things (John 14:26), and guide us into all truth (16:13). Jesus condensed all 613 laws of Judaism into two basic laws to apply to mankind:

> Jesus said to him, "'You shall love the LORD your God with all your heart, with all your soul, and with all your mind.' This is the first and great commandment. And the second is like it: 'You shall love your neighbor as yourself.' On these two commandments hang all the Law and the Prophets."
>
> —MATTHEW 22:37–40

Just these two should keep us out of trouble for a lifetime.

When I was growing up and would question my mother about why I had to do something she told me to do, her final statement would be, "Because I said so!" That was the end of the discussion. In the same manner, we can believe the Bible "because God said so!"

Find the answer in His Word before you pray, then present your case to the Lord, in accordance with His instructions: "Come now, and let us reason together" (Isa. 1:18). You are basing your plea on what He has already said, and because He said so, you can rest on 1 John 5:14–15:

> Now this is the confidence that we have in Him, that if we ask anything according to His will, He hears us. And if we know that He hears us, whatever we

ask, we know that we have the petitions that we have asked of Him.

There is the question of the fullness of God's time for the answer to be manifested, but even in the waiting we are blessed, because:

> Those who wait on the LORD Shall renew their strength; They shall mount up with wings like eagles, They shall run and not be weary, They shall walk and not faint.
>
> —ISAIAH 40:31

As we wait, we must be about our Father's business; and as we are about His business, He will be about ours. We don't "hang in there;" we "stand on the promises." James warns that he who doubts is a double-minded man, unstable in all his ways, and he will not receive anything from the Lord (James 1:6–8).

A dear friend of mine was diagnosed with breast cancer, which can be a very frightening thing, but she did not miss a beat. She had a lumpectomy, went through the chemo and radiation treatments, and now is on oral medication. All this time, she continued singing in the choir, serving on various committees and even ministering and encouraging another cancer patient in her congregation. Her attitude and demeanor through this ordeal has been a witness to her friends, coworkers, and especially to her church. When someone asked how she was able to come through all this, her answer was, "Standing on the promises!"

The Virgin Mary was overwhelmed when Gabriel appeared to her and said, "Rejoice, highly favored one, the Lord is with you; blessed are you among women!" (Luke 1:28). He went on to say that she would bear a son; his name would be Jesus, the Son of the Most High God. She was to be the mother of the long awaited Messiah. Incredible as it seemed, Mary believed. When she went to visit her relative Elizabeth, who was bearing in her womb John the Baptist, the messenger of Jesus, Baby John leaps for joy within her womb, and Elizabeth proclaims: "Blessed is she who believed, for there will be a fulfillment of those things which were told her from the Lord" (v. 45). Because God said so!

Walter Cronkite was a longtime news commentator on radio and television from 1937 to 1981. He was an anchor man on CBS television for almost twenty years, during which time polls voted him the most trusted man in America. He would close his broadcast with the words: "And that's the way it is."[1]

How much more should we trust and listen to our Father God, who is *the* Commentator above all commentators. It is His Word that we must heed. "And the Word [Jesus] became flesh and dwelt among us, and we beheld His glory, the glory as of the only begotten of the Father, full of grace and truth" (John 1:14). It doesn't take a rocket scientist to figure this out; actually, it's very simple.

## IT'S SO SIMPLE

Do you have questions—things you don't know?
Jesus is the Answer—to Him you should go.

Are you thirsty and dry, like parched land?
He's the Living Water; He'll help you stand.

Are you hungry—in need of food?
He's the Bread of Life—so tasty and good.

Are you weary—in need of rest?
He's your Peace; in Him you are blessed.

Are you lost—in need of a Guide?
He's the Way—in Him abide.

All that you need, He will supply,
Generously and abundantly, on Him rely.

For in His Word you'll find the answers ring true.
Jesus—the Way, the Truth and the Life—and He's
    waiting for you.

Call on His Name and from your struggling cease,
He'll be the Anchor of your soul, and bring Perfect
    Peace.

In contrast we have the doubters like the disciple Thomas. He was not with the other disciples on the day of resurrection so he did not see the risen Christ, and he did not believe their report. Jesus had told the disciples on three separate occasions that He would be crucified, but He would rise again on the third day (Matt. 16:21; Mark 10:32–34; Luke 18:32–33). Luke goes into further explanation: "But they understood none of these things; his saying was hidden from them, and they did not know the things which were spoken" (18:34). They had ears, but did not hear; they did not comprehend. Perhaps if they had perceived the advance warning, they would have botched God's plan. It does seem too good to be true: that Jesus, the Son of God, would pay such a costly price for our redemption from sin—amazing grace!

Bless Thomas' heart! It must grieve our Lord when we are unbelieving believers, yet He always gives us another chance. Jesus came to Thomas personally post-resurrection. "Then

He said to Thomas, 'Reach your finger here, and look at My hands; and reach our hand here, and put it into My side. Do not be unbelieving, but believing.' And Thomas answered and said to Him, 'My Lord and My God!'" (John 20:27–28). He was the first disciple to give the title of "God" to Jesus.

History records that Thomas evangelized in Syria and present day Iran, and finally to the Christians in the Malabar coast area of India. Tradition holds that he was martyred by spearing, near Madras in AD 72, and was buried at Mylapore, a suburb of that city. Thomas ended well.[2]

We had an exchange student from Sweden live with us for a year (1981–1982). She attended her senior year of high school with my middle son and daughter, who were juniors. She was active in school activities and went to Sunday school, church, and Methodist Youth Fellowship. She even went with our family on weekend lay witness missions to various Methodist churches in Georgia. As her time with us was coming to a close, her family, consisting of her father, mother, and brother, came for a short visit. They, too, went to church with us and we did the usual tourist sites; it was a delightful time. I especially remember with fondness the mom and dad attending the Sunday school class that I taught. We always had the blessing at meal times; our faith was open, no holding back. The family returned home, and as I was driving our student (now like a daughter to me) to the airport for her flight back to Sweden, I lamented that she had never accepted Christ into her heart. She just patted me lovingly on the knee, saying she was just "too technical." She has come back for visits many times, has married and now has a daughter of her own. As of this writing, she is still "too technical." But she came to us for a reason, and that seed we planted is still growing, despite all technicalities. God's Word never returns void (Isa. 55:11).

# THE DOUBTER

God is just and God is fair,
Evidence of Him is everywhere!
The doubter asks for a sign,
Just show me a miracle—then I'll resign.
God answered that prayer long ago
When He hung in the sky a rainbow.

The doubter says, "I'm more technical than that,"
So God gives him a television set.
The doubter replies, "That came from man,"
And God says, "Yes, and I made man!"

And I made the fire, the wind, and the rain,
And I made the car, the train, and the plane—
From the flea to the horse to the elephant,
From the tent to the house to the monument.
Look all around you, doubter, and see
Everything was made by Me.

And I gave you a mind with which to doubt,
To reason and think, to ask questions about,
And I gave you a heart, a mind and a soul,
And I AM the One who makes you whole.

It grieves My heart when you question Me,
For I gave My life to set you free,
To claim victory for you on Calvary
So you can live eternally with Me.

I patiently wait at the door of your heart
But I cannot come in unless you invite.
Lay aside your doubts, open the door wide
So that your Savior, Teacher, and Friend can come
      inside.

Then together we will walk on this path toward
    home;
You'll find that I AM the answer to the questions
    you pose.

# Chapter 3
## Spec-Tater

**S**OME TATERS HAVE "eyes," and we call them "spec-taters." By definition, a spectator is an onlooker, one who beholds or observes. They are quite necessary, especially at sporting events; if they did not pay an admission, there would be no game. Someone has to pay for the uniforms, coaches, rent, and salaries. If not for the fans, there would be no one to cheer. Where would the fun be? What would be the point?

Infants are precious as they begin to crawl, stand alone, and then walk. Even at that early stage, they want attention. "Look at me! I'm something special! I'm so smart!" They are performing and need spectators to applaud and encourage them to go forward—to reach for the stars. We never really outgrow that need for praise. If we do not get that affirmation, we become stunted in our growth.

As we mature, we learn that while there is a time to look (be a spectator), there is also a time to act (be a participator). Perhaps King Solomon should have added that to his list in Ecclesiastes 3:1–8 when he said that there is a season for everything and "a time for every purpose under heaven" (v. 1).

There is a sad account in Genesis 19 of a time when Lot, the nephew of Abraham, was warned by two angels that the city of Sodom was about to be destroyed. He, his wife, and his two daughters must leave immediately or they would perish. However, Lot lingered. The angels brought them outside the city and cautioned them not to look back, but Lot's wife "looked back from behind him, and she became a pillar of salt" (Gen. 19:26). Jesus admonishes us: "Remember Lot's wife" (Luke 17:32). We can see the lesson of not looking back, not dwelling on the past, in the design of our automobiles today. The front windshield is infinitely larger than the rear view mirror.

Jesus was talking to a man who wanted to become His disciple, but the man said that he first had to go home and say goodbye to his family. Jesus replied, "No one, having put his hand to the plow, and looking back, is fit for the kingdom of God" (Luke 9:62). We are called to make the Lord our top priority. If you know anything about farming, you know you cannot plow a straight furrow if you are constantly looking back.

Paul wrote an encouraging letter to the believers at Philippi, the first Christians in Europe, wherein he admonished them to keep looking forward, saying,

> Brethren, I do not count myself to have apprehended; but one thing I do, forgetting those things which are behind and reaching forward to those things which are ahead, I press forward to the goal for the prize of the upward call of God in Christ Jesus.
> —PHILIPPIANS 3:13–14

They respected and honored Paul; he was a spiritual father to them and they are touched when he tells them that he, too, is a work in progress. He has not fully arrived, but he is on the road; and as he is pressing forward, he must forget "those things which are behind."

Sometimes we are like baby eagles; we love our comfortable, downy nests and we want to stay there. However,

Mama Eagle one day pulls out the fluffy feathers and the twigs underneath cause pain. Then Mama pushes the eaglets out of the nest, causing them to tumble toward the earth; but she sweeps under them, bearing them up on her wings. Thus she is teaching them to fly and to trust she will keep them from falling.

My son Scott had a similar experience. His wife gave him a free fall jump from an airplane for his birthday. Heights are not Scott's favorite thing, but there was no way he could decline such a unique gift, much less show his fear. His family came out to cheer him on, and he bravely smiled as he waved to us what he thought could be his last goodbye. We watched the plane as it ascended, and Scott as he descended. We ran to him with our congratulations, but he could not stop talking; he was so pumped, so excited. Hugging his wife, he exclaimed, "I want to do it again!"

## JUMP

It's so high—that never-ending sky—
Stretched from here to there—
Acres and acres of pure blue air.

I am to leave my safe terrain,
And fly in this snub-nosed plane.
I am to jump with this little backpack,
And trust the chute will open and bring me back
Safely to the ground to the ones I love.

I shake my head—then someone gives me a shove,
And I am flying like a bird through space;
But, strangely enough, I have a smile on my face.
That was great—let's do it again!
I have faced fear and conquered him.

What I dreaded has filled me with delight,
And I learned a valuable lesson from my flight.

Don't let fear rob you of joy.
Face life like a man, not a boy.
There are times in your life when you must jump,
And trust in the Lord to bring triumph.
You have His Word on which to rely;
He calls you to be like an eagle—and FLY!

The past can tie you down—like running the race with shackles on your ankles. Paul is instructing the Christians to be free, to forgive their offenders so they can be free themselves. Jesus had taught the disciples to pray: "And forgive us our debts, As we forgive our debtors" (Matt. 6:12). In the same manner we forgive others, we ourselves are forgiven by the Father. If we withhold our forgiveness, we are setting ourselves above God, who freely forgives when we ask. Even from the cross, Jesus forgave those who nailed Him there: "Father, forgive them, for they do not know what they do" (Luke 23:34). We forgive in order to be obedient to our Lord, but also to be free ourselves. But there is more reason to forgive: it frees God to work in the life of the offender, and it irks the devil!

I can personally testify that this "forgiveness" stuff works because it did in my own life. When my husband Bob left home and divorced me after twenty-eight years of marriage, I was devastated. My heart was shattered into a zillion pieces, and I could see no future for me as a divorcee with three children. Even in my brokenness, I knew I must forgive Bob as an act of my will, so I asked the Lord to work it through me and to take any bitterness out of me—and He did. There were occasions when the enemy would try to take me captive, but each time I just forgave again and it slowly became a nonissue in my life. I was able to "reach forward to those things which are ahead" (Phil. 3:13).

The enemy has been compared to a bird building a nest. He keeps coming at you with those negative thoughts, but you must resist him and refuse to allow him to build a nest in your head. The battle is in the mind as he tries to capture your heart.

Many years ago when I worked in downtown Atlanta, I would eat in a little fast-food restaurant. It had a sign that amused me, and yet it had a message: "As you travel on through life, brother, whatever be your goal, keep your eye on the doughnut, and not on the hole!"

I interpreted this to mean that I must stay focused on my goal (the doughnut), which was positive, and not on the negative (the hole). Forgiveness is positive; unforgiveness is negative. The Lord has blessed my life in allowing me to go on many mission trips for Him, and I have even written about that in my first book, *Around the World in Seventy Years.*[1] Those doors would not have opened for me had I not forgiven Bob because "those things behind" would have kept me bound. I would still be focused on the "hole" instead of being the "whole" person I am today. However, like Paul, I am still a work in progress.

Peter learned the hard way about keeping your focus. After feeding the five thousand, Jesus sent the disciples to go before Him to the other side of the lake while He dismissed the crowd and took some time to pray. A sudden storm arose and the boat was being tossed by the waves. Jesus approached them, walking on the water. (See Matthew 14:13–27.) Peter cried out to Jesus:

> "Lord, if it is You, command me to come to You on the water." So He said, "Come." And when Peter had

come down out of the boat, he walked on the water to go to Jesus. But when he saw that the wind was boisterous, he was afraid, and beginning to sink he cried out, saying "Lord, save me!" And immediately Jesus stretched out His hand and caught him, and said to him, "O you of little faith, why did you doubt?"
—Matthew 14:28–31

Peter moved his focus from Jesus to his circumstances—the boisterous winds, waves, and water. But you have to admire Peter; he got out of the boat. The other eleven did not; they chose to trust in the boat. For a time Peter was trusting Jesus to walk on the water; and at the time he was going under the water, he knew to call on Jesus for his salvation.

We also know that Peter's "little faith" grew. In the very next chapter of Matthew, Jesus asked the disciples:

"Who do men say that I, the Son of Man, am?" ... Simon Peter answered and said, "You are the Christ, the Son of the living God." Jesus answered and said unto him, "Blessed are you, Simon Bar-Jonah, for flesh and blood has not revealed this to you, but My Father who is in heaven. And I say to you that you are Peter, and on this rock I will build My church, and the gates of Hades shall not prevail against it."
—Matthew 16:13, 16–18

Peter made quite a comeback, which gives us hope when our faith seems small.

The other part of that "one thing" was to reach "forward to those things which are ahead." Poet Robert Browning wrote, "Ah, but a man's reach should exceed his grasp, or what's a heaven for?"[2]

What we have accomplished is in our grasp; we hold it in our hand. But we were made for more; therefore, we keep reaching forward to fulfill our destinies. Scripture warns: "Where there is no vision, the people perish" (Prov. 29:18, KJV).

Habakkuk the prophet was pleading with God to send revival. At the conclusion of his prayer, he said he was going to watch and see what the Lord had to say and he was willing to be corrected (Hab. 2:1). Continuing in verses 2 and 3:

> Then the LORD answered me and said: "Write the vision plain on tablets, That he may run who reads it. For the vision is yet for an appointed time; But at the end it will speak, and it will not lie. Though it tarries, wait for it; Because it will surely come, it will not tarry."

The Lord is instructing Habakkuk to write the vision in big letters so even the person running by would not miss it. The picture in our mind would be a jogger running past a huge billboard with a sign of such proportions that the runner could keep running without breaking stride and still read the words. The Lord also tells Habakkuk that the vision will be fulfilled at His appointed time and cautions him to wait because it will come right on time.

These verses from Habakkuk were given to me by the Holy Spirit when my husband left in 1978; from time to time I would hear them quoted in sermons or testimonies, and I was encouraged to keep waiting. If I had given up, I would not have received my miracle of restoration thirty years later. Take heart, dear reader, your "vision will be fulfilled" in God's appointed time and it will be sweet.

Jacob used this "billboard" principle in Genesis 30. He

had worked for his father-in-law, Laban, for many years; and now he wanted to return home with his family and livestock. Laban knows he has been blessed because of Jacob so he does not want Jacob to leave. Laban is willing to pay Jacob any wages he asks, and the deal is made that Jacob would "pass through all your [Laban's] flock today, removing from there all the speckled and spotted sheep, and all the brown ones among the lambs, and the spotted and speckled among the goats; and these shall be my [Jacob's] wages" (Gen. 30:32).

Jacob then separated his speckled and spotted sheep and goats, and the brown lambs, and put some distance between his livestock and that of Laban. Then Jacob made his "billboards" and put them in strategic places. Read in Genesis 30:37–43:

> Now Jacob took for himself rods of green poplar and of the almond and chestnut trees, peeled white strips in them, and exposed the white which was in the rods. And the rods which he had peeled, he set before the flocks in the gutters, in the watering troughs where the flocks came to drink, so that they should conceive when they came to drink. So the flocks conceived before the rods, and the flocks brought forth streaked, speckled, and spotted Then Jacob separated the lambs, and made the flocks face toward the streaked and all the brown in the flock of Laban; but he put his own flocks by themselves and did not put them with Laban's flock. And it came to pass, whenever the stronger livestock conceived, that Jacob placed the rods before the eyes of the livestock in the gutters, that they might conceive among the rods. But when the flocks were feeble, he did not put them in; so the feebler were Laban's and the stronger

Jacob's. Thus the man became exceedingly prosperous, and had large flocks, female and male servants, and camels and donkeys.

There is the expected confrontation between Laban and Jacob, resulting in a peace covenant. Jacob had been obedient to the instructions of God when He said in Genesis 31:12–13:

> Lift your eyes now and see, all the rams which leap on the flocks are streaked, speckled, and gray-spotted... I am the God of Bethel, where you anointed the pillar and where you made a vow to Me. Now arise, get out of this land, and return to the land of your family.

Jacob returned home, in the fullness of God's time. He went out empty but he came home full.

Before we were even a glimmer in our earthly father's eyes, our heavenly Father had unique plans for each one of His children: "For we are His workmanship, created in Christ Jesus for good works, which God prepared beforehand that we should walk in them" (Eph. 2:10). Forgive me, dear reader, if I use this scripture more than once; it's one of my favorites—a life verse. Another great one is Jeremiah 29:11: "For I know the thoughts that I think toward you, says the LORD, thoughts of peace and not of evil, to give you a future and a hope." Feel free to stand on them; I do, and there is plenty of room.

Since our lives are planned, it follows that we can expect God to move in "extra-ordinary" ways in the midst of what we may consider to be ordinary, all the time working for our good (Rom. 8:28) and advancing His kingdom. Our Lord is always up to something. I give you a personal example:

# AN ORDINARY DAY—FRAGILE: HANDLE WITH CARE

It was just an ordinary day,
No foreboding of what was coming my way.
I had said my prayers, put my armor on,
So what could possibly go wrong?

There is a God on high and nothing escapes His eye;
He stirred up His saints to pray; had His angels on
    stand-by.
The van was aimed at me like a weapon of mass
    destruction—
The red light at the intersection causing no
    hesitation.

This was no ordinary day!

My little blue car shot across four lanes of traffic,
Spinning into a clump of trees—it was like magic!
Four witnesses made upright the car—
Firemen, police and medics—I was the star!

The doctor with x-rays in hand gave a good report—
Once again the Lord had shielded me—had been my
    Fort.
What could have been a great tragedy
Was transformed into a testimony!

It was an "extra-ordinary" day!

# Chapter 4
# PARTICIPA-TATER

HE FOLLOWERS OF Christ were admonished by James, the half-brother of Jesus and leader of the church in Jerusalem, to "be doers of the word, and not hearers only" (James 1:22), because "faith without works is dead" (2:20). Thus, we move from being "spec-taters" into being "participators." (I would say "participa-taters" to carry out the theme, but it trips my tongue!)

The words of James might have been the inspiration for an advertising campaign of Nike, the shoe and sportswear company, which caused their business to boom. The highly recognized logo of the company is the "Swoosh" (looks like a check mark). Above the swoosh is the name "Nike," which in Greek means "victory," and under the swoosh in capital letters it says JUST DO IT.[1]

I can relate to that because I know we were created to do good works (remember Ephesians 2:10). I have a picture in my mind of a spreadsheet in heaven with my name at the top. Below are listed all the things assigned for me to accomplish before I leave earth. As I complete each one, there is a checkmark. When all my assignments are completed and checked off, it will be time for me to graduate, go home to heaven, kick back, and prop my feet on the front porch banister of my mansion in glory (John 14:2).

I asked the Lord once to show me what my mansion looks like, and in my mind's eye I saw a white colonial two-story house with white columns and rockers on the wide porch that extended across the front. Lush green grass (that never needs mowing) covered the lawn, and there was a wide border of white Shasta daisies down the sides and at the front of my property. I couldn't see them, but I knew there was a beautiful rose garden in the rear and a lake.

A friend of mine said she did not care about a mansion in glory—a log cabin in the sky was fine with her. I know any log cabin our Lord provides will be spectacular, but since we serve the Lord God Almighty who owns all the gold and silver, the cattle on a thousand hills, and the treasures of the deep, why not go for the mansion? Of course, just being in His presence would be bliss, even if it meant camping out in a pup tent!

I have been taught that you cannot take anything to heaven with you, except people, but you can send your treasures on ahead. Jesus said:

> Do not lay up for yourselves treasures on earth, where moth and rust destroy and where thieves break through and steal; but lay up for yourselves treasures in heaven, where neither moth nor rust destroys and where thieves do not break in and steal. For where your treasure is, there your heart will be also.
>
> —MATTHEW 6:19–21

The story is told of a rich church lady who died and went to heaven. St. Peter was escorting her to her new home and she was excited. However, when they arrived at a lean-to shack, she was puzzled. "This can't be my home in glory," she cried. St. Peter replied, "I'm sorry, Ma'am; but this is all you sent us to work with."

When a real estate developer takes out a construction loan with the bank, he is given an account on which he draws to pay the building expenses. Does that apply to Christians here on earth? When we tithe, give offerings, support missionaries, make charitable contributions, or exercise "pure and undefiled religion" in visiting orphans and widows in trouble (James 1:27); or when we minister as unto Jesus by feeding the hungry, giving water to the thirsty, taking in the stranger, clothing the naked, and visiting the prisoner (Matt. 25:35–40), are we thus "laying up treasure in heaven?" The qualifier must be that we are doing these things from a heart of love for the Master, not to stack up Brownie points and get a payback. It must be all about Jesus, not about "self." Just as He was a Man about others, our call is the same because people matter to God.

Let's take a short trip here (my Sunday school class would call it a "rabbit trail"). I want to take you to Alaska because I am still so full of the wonder of it that I just cannot keep it to myself! My son-in-law/love, Russell, and his wife, who is my daughter, Stacey, took the moms on a cruise to Alaska. Russell was keeping a promise to his dad, who died almost a year ago, to take his mom on trips because she had spent so many years as his caregiver. I was invited because I live in the mother-in-law suite in the basement of their home (actually, they live in my attic is the way I look at it) and there was no polite way to leave me out, since I have "passport—will travel" at any opportunity. Also, I am richly blessed and favored by God! Gladys and I would be roommates, and hopefully keep each other out of trouble. Though I had been "around the world in seventy years," I had never been on a cruise, and my prior accommodations had been a bit more primitive.

During my trip I kept a journal and took notes (part of who I am) on lectures given by rangers and tour guides, so I have a first-hand account with which to take you along on my adventure. It took three airplanes to get us from Atlanta to Seattle to Anchorage to Fairbanks. Then we drove to Denali, a national park area covering approximately 6.5 million acres—yes, *million*! Our first day we took a bus ride through a portion of the park; there was so much to see and to learn from God's creation.

There was a little bird sitting in the tip-top of a tree; it was Alaska's state bird, the Willow Ptarmigan. This gutsy bird is very clever and courageous. His mate stays in the nest in the middle boughs, along with the babies, while he stands watch. When a predator approaches, he flies toward the enemy like a suicide bomber, and then he veers off, lands on the ground, and pretends to have a broken wing. He uses this ruse to take the enemy away from the nest, chasing him instead of Mrs. Ptarmigan; thus protecting his family. It doesn't matter that he's just a small bird facing gigantic odds; he wins because he does not allow himself to be the "victim" but the "victor."

This little bird also reminded me of the account of David versus Goliath in 1 Samuel 17, especially verse 48, when "David hurried and ran toward the army to meet the Philistine." Continuing in verse 51:

> Therefore David ran and stood over the Philistine, took his sword and drew it out of its sheath and killed him, and cut off his head with it. And when the Philistines saw that their champion was dead, they fled.

David was victorious because he came "in the name of the LORD of Hosts, the God of the armies of Israel" (v. 45). We likewise are victorious because our Lord Jesus Christ promised:

> All authority has been given to Me in heaven and on
> earth. Go therefore and make disciples of all nations,
> baptizing them in the name of the Father and of the
> Son and of the Holy Spirit, teaching them to observe
> all things I have commanded you; and lo, I am with
> you always, even to the end of the age.
>
> —MATTHEW 28:18–20

We have been given His authority and the power to use the name of the Father, the Son and the Holy Spirit. Additionally, we have the promise of His presence with us as we carry out this Great "Co-Mission."

We saw many other birds and animals in Denali, including eagles, sheep, caribou, moose, bears, and even a red fox. There were glaciers, and the majestic Mt. McKinley towered over everything. This is the tallest mountain in North America, standing 20,320 feet high. It can be seen as far away as Anchorage. You just don't run up to this mountain and start climbing. It takes great preparation and training. You must have some other mountains under your belt before you are allowed to even attempt this climb. Plus you take the climb in stages, allowing your body to adjust to the altitude. You also need adequate supplies, such as proper clothing, water, food and even a can for your body wastes. After you reach the top (sadly, few do), you cannot just do a victory dance and run to the bottom. You must come down in stages, carrying everything with you, even the potty can. You are to leave no "footprints."

What is the lesson here? The highest mountain can be overcome if you are properly prepared and equipped and if you have patience and perseverance. As Christians we have available to us the whole armor of God, which includes the girdle of truth, the breastplate of righteousness, boots of the gospel of peace, shield of faith, helmet of salvation, the sword of the Spirit (Word of God), and above all, prayer and supplication in the Spirit (Eph. 6:14–18). We are guaranteed that no weapon formed against us will prosper (Isa. 54:17). We have all the time we need because we have been given eternal life (1 John 5:11). We simply put one foot in front of the other and breathe in and breathe out long enough (persevere), and thus we overcome the adversary.

An especially outstanding event was the day our ship entered Glacier Bay. Park Rangers came on board to teach us about the glaciers; all that information that leaves you speechless. Less than 200 years ago, all this land was covered in ice. The glaciers, these rivers of ice, have been, for the most part, slowly receding. We heard and watched them "calving." Huge blocks of ice break off with a loud cry; the small icebergs hit the water and float downstream. Some of the glaciers were of a bluish tint, changing the color of the water around them to turquoise. You could see streaks of blue in the icebergs as well. However, some glaciers were gray and black because of the soil they move with them.

What I saw here was God moving slowly and persistently through time, continuing His creation as He uses rivers of ice to carve out valleys, filling them with water and exposing huge mountains, granite cliffs, and waterfalls, giving His creatures more land in which to multiply and thrive. I felt so tiny and at the same time so important because *my* heavenly Father let me witness His handiwork. He made it for my pleasure and enjoyment; and yet I have a duty and responsibility to honor and preserve my part as best I can.

The Lord gave me a special treat on another afternoon when I was on the top deck of the cruise ship (14th floor). I had gone alone and some fellow passengers were standing at the rail admiring some eagles that were flying below us a short distance away, closer to the shore.

I have long admired eagles because, like the Ptarmigan, they are courageous. When they see a storm coming, they set their wings and fly into it, letting the air currents lift them above the tumult. In Isaiah 40:31 The Lord promises:

> But those who wait on the LORD Shall renew their strength; They shall mount up with wings like eagles, They shall run and not be weary, They shall walk and not faint.

To "wait" means not to just fold your arms, sit back, and watch time tick by; but it means to serve, like waiting on tables. I stood on this promise when my husband left; I "waited" for his return, and as I waited the Lord kept "renewing." Therefore, eagles are special to me. Now back to the ship.

All the people who had been standing there with me left, leaving me alone. I kept watching the eagles, and then one veered off and headed straight toward me. I could actually see his face, and I thought he was going to hit me. But then he swooped up, and I saw him against the backdrop of the blue sky—wings outspread and his head pointed toward space. Wow! The Lord had sent an eagle, just for me. Lavish love!

The Lord kept showing up and showing off. We went on an excursion into Juneau to go whale watching on a small boat. As we got out into the bay, we saw other boats circled around, which meant whales had been spotted. Some of us went on the top deck to get a better view. We saw water spouts shooting up from approximately eighteen whales as they swam in a circle, came up out of the water, then dived down to "bubble feed," trapping the fish. They would then spring up again, with huge mouths open to catch the fish, and then breach, with tails hitting the water and causing big splashes. If my arms had been a bit longer, I would have been able to touch the side of one of these big ones. The captain was beside himself, exclaiming that this was a once in a two-lifetime event!

Let's come down from this epic episode and return to Denali for a poignant moment. As we were leaving the area, we spotted a caribou with large antlers grazing not far from the road. Its rear right leg seemed to be injured, perhaps even broken, and it was trying to bow its head and get the leg between the antlers so it could jerk the leg back into place. It tried again and again, but to no avail. This was breaking our hearts because no one could help. The guide said that the caribou had little to no chance of survival since the wolves would surely come. The rangers would not intervene as the policy was to let nature take its course. I prayed that Jesus would come and heal this caribou; that in some miraculous way the leg would go back into place. When there is nothing we can do in the natural, we can always pray and trust in the goodness of our God. Actually, prayer and trust should come first in any event.

I came home from Alaska with my cup overflowing with joy and wonder at our Creator God, who has done and is continually doing awesome feats. I especially loved these wide-open spaces of nature and how the folks in Alaska are seeking to preserve their environment.

A few weeks after the Alaska trip, I was blessed to go to Dollywood in the Grand Smoky Mountains of Tennessee. My granddaughter Abby had a summer job as a tram operator and was concurrently serving with The Navigators, a Christian organization working with college students. We had a cabin on the side of a mountain and could look out over the valley, which was dotted with other cabins. At the base we could see the neon lights of all the business establishments. One morning we hiked to Grotto Falls, which was so beautiful, but as the day wore on, it became crowded with people. We drove back through Gatlinburg, which has businesses built right up to the edge of the river and there are people everywhere.

When we returned to our cabin, I stood on the porch, just thinking of the contrast between Alaska and Gatlinburg and Dollywood. I thought about the sheer beauty of Mt. McKinley, how important it is to so many (as are Gatlinburg and Dollywood) as tourist attractions. God has given us nature, His creation, to draw us unto Himself, and it is a good thing that people flock to marvel at His handiwork because it is one of the methods He uses to show us His reality. And I thought especially about majestic Mt. McKinley. However, if you were to take a freckle-faced little boy of about six or seven with some of his baby teeth missing and dressed in a T-shirt, jeans, and sneakers with his baseball hat on backwards, he would be much more glorious than Mt. McKinley because he is God's crowning achievement. Now, just replace this little guy with yourself; because you, too, are a trophy of His grace—unique, one-of-a-kind, and you are so dear to the Creator's heart.

We are called to be participators, to take part in this circle of love and pass the good news on to others. It's too good to keep to ourselves!

## GOD SO LOVED THE WORLD

God so loved the world that He sent,
Jesus so loved the world that He went,
Holy Spirit so loved the world that He remains,
Equipping the saints to advance the Kingdom's
domain.

I'm to so love the world that I go,
Sharing the gospel with all on earth here below.
Shout the news both near and far—
Jesus loves you, just the way you are!

Your Father has a mansion for you in glory,
In the Bible is written the sublimest of stories—
How Jesus stands at the door of your heart,
To open the door and say "yes" is the easy part.

The Holy Spirit will guide you as you walk the walk,
And stand at the door of your mouth as you talk the
talk.
Angels will guard you with their great strength and
skill,
So the enemy cannot come against you at his will.

The promise is true; God's love is for you.
He delights to give you His best—
Jesus, His Son, Who came for everyone!
Don't delay—today say "YES!"

Chapter 5

# GIFTS

**M**Y SALVATION WAS "the gift of God" (Rom. 6:23), but it is my joy and honor to be a "doer" (James 1:22) of the Word, *plus* there are awesome "perks" that accrue to me and to you as kingdom kids, such as gifts, rewards, and crowns.

When Jesus ascended into heaven, He gave us gifts. You would think He had done enough: leaving a throne in glory and coming down to earth to ransom us from the clutches of Satan through His crucifixion and resurrection; showing us how to walk in victory over sin, death, and the grave; and giving us the sure promise of His return for His bride, the church. It's just like our Jesus to always give more. In Ephesians 4:7–8, we read:

> But to each one of us grace was given according to the measure of Christ's gift. Therefore He says: "When He ascended on high, He led captivity captive, And gave gifts to men."

Continuing in verses 11–13:

> And He Himself gave some to be apostles, some prophets, some evangelists, and some pastors and teachers, for the equipping of the faith and of the knowledge of the Son of God, to a perfect man, to the measure of the stature of the fullness of Christ.

Paul says that we as believers have different gifts—special callings on each individual:

> For as we have many members in one body, but all members do not have the same function, so we, being many, are one body in Christ, and individually members of one another. Having then gifts differing according to the grace that is given to us, let us use them: if prophecy, let us prophesy in proportion to our faith; or ministry, let us use it in our ministering; he who teaches, in teaching; he who exhorts, in exhortation; he who gives, with liberality; he who leads, with diligence; he who shows mercy, with cheerfulness.
>
> —ROMANS 12:4–8

Paul goes on to say that he does not want us to be ignorant concerning spiritual gifts (1 Cor. 12:1). He goes into further detail:

> There are diversities of gifts, but the same Spirit. There are differences of ministries, but the same Lord. And there are diversities of activities, but it is the same God who works all in all. But the manifestation of the Spirit is given to each one for the profit of all: for to one is given the word of wisdom through the Spirit, to another the word of knowledge through the same Spirit, to another faith by the same Spirit, to another gifts of healing by the same Spirit, to another the working of miracles, to another prophecy, to another discerning of spirits, to another different kinds of tongues, to another the interpretation of tongues. But one and the same Spirit works all these things, distributing to each one individually as He wills.
>
> —1 CORINTHIANS 12:4–11

We even have a guarantee on the gifts. Our Lord promised that He would not give a gift and then take it back. He won't say, "Just kidding!" He affirms that "the gifts and the calling of God are irrevocable" (Rom. 11:29). *Plus*, there is an added bonus: His gifts are good and perfect (James 1:17).

A friend of mine was experiencing the recurrence of cancer. For a second time she faced the ordeal of chemo treatments, yet she had a supernatural peace; her *"knower" knew* that her healing would be manifested in the fullness of God's time. The Holy Spirit had given her the gift of faith. She endured the treatments but used this time to witness for the Lord. Her son went with her one day per week. Now that chemo has ended, they are both missing that time and the special people they met. She is now cancer free; and all those who love her, including her doctor, are praising the Lord.

That same gift was given to me when the Lord promised to walk with me after my husband left, promising that when I reached the other side there would be restoration. During those waiting years, I would receive signs of encouragement, enabling me to wait upon the Lord. Actually, I have three specific things that make my faith antenna to kick into alert: rainbows, pennies, and birds on telephone wires.

The rainbow is the sign of the everlasting covenant promise God made with Noah that he would never again destroy the earth by flood (Gen. 9:11–13). God said, "It shall be, when I bring a cloud over earth, that the rainbow shall be seen in the cloud; and I will remember My covenant which is between Me and you and every living creature of all flesh" (Gen. 9:14–15). Therefore, when I see a rainbow over the "cloud" in my life, my Lord is in essence saying that He remembers His promise to me. With my husband it was the promise of restoration; other times it concerns promises in His Word of healing, provision, or whatever my need is at that time.

There was one particular occasion when I needed confirmation about a move I believed I was to make, so I asked the Lord to give me a rainbow. When I met my daughter after her work at the mall, the sky was very dark and there was a rainbow stretched across the horizon. She said, "Mom! Have you ever seen such a "mo-ka" (her slang word for massive, huge, big) rainbow?" I had my answer.

Another time, I dreamed I was in the plaza of a Mexican village. There was a cantina with a neon sign on the roof that was pulsating the rainbow. It was like the Lord was saying, "See this! See this! See this!" Wow! I assume, dear reader, that you get my message: I love rainbows. The next time you see one, just know that your Lord is remembering His promises to you.

Pennies are dropped by angels to remind us to trust in God; I have heard this saying all my life, but I cannot remember the source. I just know that it is true. Someone recently told me that if the penny is face up, that mean's good luck; if face down, that's bad. I do not believe in "luck," as that is short for Lucifer, and he has no place in me "because He who is in you is greater than he who is in the world" (1 John 4:4).

I can prove that the only thing that matters is that the penny is inscribed with "In God We Trust." On a recent trip to Great Lakes for the graduation of my grandson Matt from Navy boot camp, I found a penny as my family and I were approaching the Atlanta airport; and, of course, I picked it up and put it in my pocket. At the check-in desk, the airline clerk requested a $25.00 baggage fee, which I said I did not owe because of my credit card; she verified this with another clerk and the fee was waived.

On the return flight to Atlanta from Chicago, I found another penny in a rain puddle. I recalled the face up, face down theory, so I noted that it was face down and it was covered in water; but I picked it up anyhow, because luck has nothing to do with me. I prefer to be blessed. Upon checking in, the clerk said I owed a $25.00 baggage fee; and I resisted, saying it had been waived before and I should not have to pay it now. She looked at a list and immediately waived the fee. Before I had time to walk away, another clerk came to tell my clerk that she had made a mistake—I did owe the $25.00. The first clerk said it was too late because it had been waived; she smiled and wished me a good trip home. My angels had saved me $50.00!

On a second Wild West trip with my family, we were at the base of Vernal Falls in Yosemite National Park. They had all hiked to the top, and I had stopped to rest at the base of the falls. I was so-o-o tired! The water was colliding with rocks, forming rainbows; I looked down at my feet and saw three pennies (Father, Son, Holy Spirit). My strong inclination had been just to wait for my family and not finish the climb to the top, but then I was inspired and started forward. My family was waving at me from the top; and as I crested the hill, they started shouting. I threw up my hands in victory! Don't forget to pick up those pennies; angels want to give you a push!

You may think it strange that birds on telephone wires can be signs of encouragement, so this is the scoop. I had been attending a certain church for a number of years and was very happy there; but during one specific Sunday sermon, I heard the Lord speak to my spirit saying, "It's time to go!" Surely this could not be the Lord, so I sought confirmation. The Lord led me to a zoning meeting, where I met the youth pastor of a church in my neighborhood who greatly impressed me. I later believed, after much prayer, that I was to go to this church. When I did, I felt at home; that this was my new assignment. Looking back, it certainly was because at that church I was able to study and obtain college credits for a double major in biblical studies and Christian counseling.

I decided to attend a women's retreat because I did not know anybody, being the "new kid," and I wanted to build relationships. I was in the cabin with women who had been with this church since its inception; they were "leaders." I was trying so hard to fit in, be one of the gang, but it was not happening. I walked out of the conference room on break from a teaching session into a small valley surrounded with high hills. Directly in front of me, at the top of the hill, was a telephone pole with three wires descending to the bottom of the hill. On the top wire, one bird was perched, and on the second line were two birds; these three birds did not move. On the third line many birds were flitting to and fro, in a frenzy.

I felt in my spirit that the three birds represented the Father, Son, and Holy Spirit—the Trinity. The Lord was saying to my heart, "You can count on Me; I am here for you. These other people will go in and out; you stay connected to Me!" I had that blessed assurance that I was doing just fine and my many years in that church were a time of much learning, growth, and sweet friendships that are still a precious part of my life today.

Peter was on the Mount of Transfiguration with James and John when they saw Jesus transfigured before them, and with Jesus appeared Moses and Elijah talking with Jesus. Then "a bright cloud covered them, and a voice from the cloud said, 'This is my Son, whom I love; with him I am well pleased. Listen to him!'" (Matt. 17:5, NIV). This was an eyewitness account, a personal experience; and it made an impact on the life of Peter. However, Peter later said there was confirmation even greater than this encounter on the Mount of Transfiguration. He wrote:

> We did not follow cleverly invented stories when we told you about the power and coming of our Lord Jesus Christ, but we were eyewitnesses of his majesty...And we have the word of the prophets made *more certain*, and you will do well to pay attention to it, as to a light shining in a dark place, until the day dawns and the morning star rises in your hearts. Above all, you must understand that no prophecy of Scripture came about by the prophet's own interpretation. For prophecy never had its origin in the will of man, but men spoke from God as they were carried along by the Holy Spirit.
>
> —2 PETER 1:16, 19–21, NIV, EMPHASIS ADDED

It is kind of our Lord to give us tangible evidence—things we can hold in our hands, like pennies; or things we can see, like rainbows, birds, telephone wires, and the like—but the best possible confirmation of His promises is His Word. He does not want us to fail the tests of life, so He has lovingly provided the answers in His Word.

Author-evangelist Marilyn Hickey once said on a television show I saw on Trinity Broadcasting Network that when we hide the word in our heart, it then goes into our mind and becomes wisdom. In Proverbs 4:7 we read that "wisdom is the principal thing."

My eldest son, Steve, was diagnosed with prostate cancer, shaking my faith foundation. Being the former legal secretary that I am, I gathered my evidence. I had three pages of healing scriptures, with many focusing on the bones because this type cancer can spread to the bones. I especially zeroed in on Ezekiel 37:3–5, wherein God commanded Ezekiel to speak to the bones and tell them to live. Jesus told the disciples in Matthew 21:21 to speak to the mountain. I presented my case to the Lord (Isa. 1:18); I spoke to the bones and told them to live; and I spoke to the cancer, commanding it to leave my son's body in the name of Jesus.

Steve had an appointment for the doctor to check his bones. Steve called me from the office, saying, "Mom, you prayed too hard; the bone was so strong that the doctor could not penetrate it!" Later Steve had robotic surgery, which resulted in no more cancer—just five little scars as reminders of what "great things" the Lord did for him (Ps. 126:2–3).

We can rest assured that when we are called, we are equipped. Our Lord would not have us be ashamed or confounded. We can be "confident of this very thing, that He who has begun a good work in you will complete it until the day of Jesus Christ" (Phil. 1:6).

All of the gifts are available to us, and the Holy Spirit will empower us with the gifts we need as we need them. There has been discussion about what is the best gift. The answer is simple: it's the one you need at that time.

However, the gifts are of no value if they are not exercised in love. Paul concludes 1 Corinthians 12 with verse 31: "But earnestly desire the best gifts. And yet I show you a more excellent way." He follows with the "love chapter" (1 Cor. 13), and in verse 13 he says: "And now abide faith, hope, love, these three; but the greatest of these is love." W. E. Vine states it this way:

> Christian love, whether exercised toward the brethren, or toward men generally, is not an impulse from the feelings, it does not always run with the natural inclinations nor does it spend itself only upon those for

whom some affinity is discovered. Love seeks the welfare of all, Rom. 15:2, and works no ill to any 13:8–10; love seeks opportunity to do good to all men and especially toward those who are of the household of the faith, Galatians 6:10. See further 1 Corinthians 13 and Colossians 3:12–14.[1]

Love is not a feeling, it is a force—the most powerful force in all the universe. God is love (1 John 4:8), and He promises that He will always be with us (Matt. 28:20). In the famous *Star Wars* movies, Han Solo says to Luke Walker, "May the Force be with you!"[2] Amen to that!

When we become a child of God, His divine love indwells us as a fruit of the Holy Spirit (Gal. 5:22). We love because we are love; it just comes naturally—like an apple tree bearing apples. When we get bumped we spill what we are full of, and "ideally" that is love. I say "ideally" because we are "Christians under construction."

## I SEE HIM!

I see my Jesus everywhere I look,
I see Him in the flowers beside the brook,
I see Him in my true love's eyes,
I see Him in the starry skies.

I hear my Jesus calling after me.
His voice rings o'er the stormy seas.
"Come, My child, and follow Me—
Together we will go through eternity."

I feel His love coming over me.
Lord, make me all I can be.
Take this nothing and make me something—
Claim me as a child of the King.

## Chapter 6
# REWARDS

**T**HE GIFTS ENABLE us to do the works, which ultimately lead to the rewards. I challenge you to check the concordance in your Bible and see the number of references to *reward*, and variances thereof, both in the Old and New Testaments.

In the Hall of Faith, Hebrews chapter 11, verses 24–26, we read:

> By faith Moses, when he became of age, refused to be called the son of Pharaoh's daughter, choosing rather to suffer affliction with the people of God than to enjoy the passing pleasures of sin, esteeming the reproach of Christ greater riches than the treasures of Egypt; for he looked to the reward.

Not just Moses, but all these heroes of the faith were looking toward the reward: Enoch, Noah, Abraham, Isaac, Jacob, Joseph, the harlot Rahab, Gideon, Barak, Samson, Jephthah, Samuel and the prophets—just to name a few.

David wrote of rewards in the Psalms. "More to be desired are they than gold, Yea, than much fine gold; Sweeter also than honey and the honeycomb. Moreover by them Your servant is warned, And in keeping them there is great reward" (Ps. 19:10–11), and "So that men will say, 'Surely there is a reward for the righteous; Surely He is God who judges in the earth'" (58:11).

King Solomon wrote: "The wicked man does deceptive work; But he who sows righteousness will have a sure reward" (Prov. 11:18), and "For so you will heap coals of fire on his head, And the LORD will reward you" (25:22).

Isaiah prophesied: "Behold, the LORD God shall come with a strong hand, And His arm shall rule for Him; Behold, His reward is with Him, And His work before Him" (Isa. 40:10).

But let's go to the Word in the New Testament. What did Jesus Himself have to say? In the Sermon on the Mount, Jesus said: "Blessed are you when they revile and persecute you, and say all kinds of evil against you falsely for My sake. Rejoice and be exceedingly glad, for great is your reward in heaven" (Matt. 5:11–12). On the other hand, "Take heed that you do not do your charitable deeds before men, to be seen by them. Otherwise, you have no reward from your Father in heaven" (Matt. 6:1).

We may think we are "giving" to others, but in reality, we are making "investments" in their lives. Jesus said,

> He who receives a prophet in the name of a prophet shall receive a prophet's reward. And he who receives a righteous man in the name of a righteous man shall receive a righteous man's reward. And whoever gives one of these little ones only a cup of cold water in the name of a disciple, assuredly, I say to you, he shall by no means lose his reward.
>
> —MATTHEW 10:41–42

Is this not laying up for ourselves treasures in heaven? (Matt. 6:20). Note also that our Lord returns "some thirtyfold, some sixty, and some a hundred" (Mark 4:8, 20). Where else could you get such a return? Only God! Jesus also commands: "Love your enemies, do good, and lend, hoping for nothing in return; and your reward will be great, and you will be sons of the Most High " (Luke 6:35).

Paul writes to the Corinthian church: "Now he who plants and he who waters are one, and each one will receive his own reward according to his own labor" (1 Cor. 3:8). He cautioned the Colossians: "Let no one cheat you of your reward, taking delight in false humility and worship of angels" (Col. 2:18).

In Hebrews 11:6 we read: "But without faith it is impossible to please Him, for he who comes to God must believe that He is, and that He is a rewarder of those who diligently seek Him."

The beloved disciple John wrote: "Look to yourselves, that we do not lose those things we worked for, but that we may receive a full reward" (2 John 1:8).

Let's go to the beginning of the Book, Genesis 15:1: "After these things the word of the Lord came to Abram in a vision, saying, 'Do not be afraid, Abram. *I am* your shield, your exceedingly great reward'" (emphasis added). Then at the end of the Book, Revelation 22:12, Jesus concludes with this great promise: "And behold *I am* coming quickly, and my reward is with Me, to give everyone according to his work" (emphasis added). When the Lord told Moses he was to lead the children of Israel out of Egypt, Moses asked the Lord what name he was to say to them. "And God said to Moses, '*I AM WHO I AM*.' And He said, 'Thus you shall say to the children of Israel, I AM has sent me to you'" (Exod. 3:14, emphasis added).

Jesus astonished the Jews who were questioning Him when He said,

"Your father Abraham rejoiced to see my day: and he saw it, and was glad." Then the Jews said to Him,

"You are not yet fifty years old, and have You seen Abraham?" Jesus said to them, "Most assuredly, I say to you, before Abraham was, I AM." Then they took up stones to throw at Him; but Jesus hid Himself and went out of the temple, going through the midst of them and so passed by.

—JOHN 8:56–58

Jesus openly declares that He is God, and the plan was to kill Him, but His time had not yet come (John 7:6). When the fullness of God's time came, He set His face like flint toward Jerusalem (Isa. 50:7; Luke 9:51).

There are many names for God: Jehovah (Self-Existing One), Jehovah Rohi (My Shepherd), Jehovah Jireh (My Provider), Jehovah Rapha (God Who Heals); Jehovah Nissi (My Banner), Jehovah Shammach (The Lord Is There), Jehovah Melek (Lord Is King), and perhaps the most tender one that Jesus used the most—Abba Father (Daddy God), and Jehovah Shalom (God of Peace). I submit that there is another that we have seen from the preceding scriptures, and that is Jehovah Shalam (My Rewarder)—Strong's #7999, similar to Jehovah Shalom (God of Peace).

There is a "hook" here, in that our motive for doing good must not be for our own benefit—to reap a reward. Peter described Jesus as one "who went about doing good" (Acts 10:38). Jesus "did not come to be served, but to serve, and to give His life a ransom for many" (Matt. 20:28). His goal was never to exalt Himself. If we should try to exalt ourselves through our pride, we most certainly will be brought low and lose our rewards. "Pride goes before destruction, And a haughty spirit before a fall" (Prov. 16:18).

Just ask the devil—pride was why he was kicked out of heaven. Satan's fall is recorded in Isaiah 14. Notice that five times Satan said "I will."

> How you are fallen from heaven, O Lucifer, son of
> the morning! How you are cut down to the ground,
> You who weakened the nations! For you have said
> in your heart: "*I will* ascend into heaven, *I will* exalt
> my throne above the stars of God; *I will* also sit on
> the mount of the congregation On the farthest sides
> of the north; *I will* ascend above the heights of the
> clouds, *I will* be like the Most High." Yet you shall
> be brought down to Sheol, To the lowest depths of
> the Pit.
> —ISAIAH 14:12–15, EMPHASIS ADDED

Satan's plan was to overthrow the "Most High," to rise to
the highest heights, but his plan was doomed to fail. Instead
of being the highest of the high, he would be the lowest of
the low. This is indeed sad in light of Satan's origin. He was
described as God's masterpiece. Ezekiel 28:12 refers to him
as "the seal of perfection, Full of wisdom and perfect in
beauty." In verse 14, he is called "the anointed cherub." He
was perfect until iniquity was found in him (v. 15); his heart
was lifted up because of his beauty, and his was wisdom
corrupted for the sake of his splendor (v. 17). In verse 19,
God calls him a "horror." How the mighty have fallen!

Jesus told the disciples, "I saw Satan fall like lightning
from heaven" (Luke 10:18). He gave the disciples another
example of a man who also had a pride problem; it is called
the "Parable of the Rich Fool," and is recorded in Luke 12:

> The ground of a certain rich man yielded plentifully.
> And he thought within himself, saying: "What shall
> I do, since I have no room to store *my* crops?" So he
> said, "I will do this: I will pull down *my* barns and
> build greater, and there I will store all *my* crops and
> all *my* goods. And I will say to *my* soul, 'Soul, you
> have many goods laid up for many years; take your

ease; eat, drink, and be merry.'" But God said to him, "Fool! This night your soul will be required of you; then whose will those things be which you have provided?" So it is with he who lays up treasure for himself, and is not rich toward God.

—LUKE 12:16–21, EMPHASIS ADDED

Did this guy have an "I-MY-ME-MINE" fixation? His life revolved around himself, his possessions, and his self-will. "I will do this, I will do that"—sounds like Satan speaking through him. James instructs: "Instead you ought to say, 'If the Lord wills, we shall live and do this or that'" (James 4:15). This puts into perspective *who* is in control: the Lord God Almighty. This is not a scary thing, but quite comforting because through the sacrifice of His Son, Jesus, we can call Him, Abba Father, Daddy God. All that power is working for our good.

Some people have difficulty in receiving from others, which actually is false humility, a form of pride. We (I'm talking about me here) love to give; it makes us feel warm and fuzzy. But we don't like to receive, because it makes us feel indebted to the giver. My sweet mother told me that I was a "bad receiver," and she could just as easily have said that I was selfish. When we don't receive gladly, we rob those persons of their blessings and joy. They are being the Lord's delivery system to get His rewards to you because you have been giving. The promise is in Luke 6:

Give, and it shall be given unto you: good measure, pressed down, and shaken together, and running over shall *men give* into your bosom. For with the same measure that you mete withal it shall be measured to you again.

—LUKE 6:38, KJV, EMPHASIS ADDED

I do volunteer work for Family Life Ministries, whose purpose is to aid the poor and needy, those in financial straits who have fallen through the cracks of society. We attempt to get donations out as fast as we receive them because we do not want to be a Dead Sea. As we give to others, we receive more. I have seen our grocery shelves almost barren; yet we pass on what we have, and always that call or delivery will come and again we will be fully stocked. We cannot hoard our "manna" because we know it will block our supply. Can you see the "circle of love" our God has established? Love in, love out—like a fresh flowing stream.

This reminds me of another children's sermon that I taught in Zimbabwe at the African church. There were approximately twenty children lined up in rows in front of me, sitting on a large mat with their legs crossed. I had some peppermint candies and was trying to teach them about passing on the love—if they gave, they would receive. It was going well as the first row kept the candy flowing; but on the second row a certain little boy decided he was going to keep all the candy, and he was stuffing his pockets. The other children were protesting, while the parents were laughing. This is so true to life:

## THE CANDY PARABLE

The little boy says, "Candy is dandy!"
"You want me to give mine away?
No way!"

The teacher says, "If you give away,
You'll receive more."
The boy shakes his head: "Give me a break;
I'm only four!"

# Chapter 7
## CROWNS

IN ADDITION TO gifts and rewards, as followers of Christ we are promised crowns. Crowns, in general, cause us to think of authority, honor, and prestige. However, there are some that we would just as soon forego, one being the crown of pride that Isaiah warns the "drunkards of Ephraim" about in Isaiah 28:1–5. We know that pride is a big "no-no" in our Lord's eyes; Satan can testify to that!

Permit me a little "rabbit trail" here. Bette Davis, the famous movie star, said, "Growing old is not for sissies."[1] But there are some perks, like senior citizen discounts and freebies. Wendy's gives seniors free drinks with their order; I actually kept my first cup for several weeks. Then the honor got old also, and I was accumulating too many to store. Then this idea came to me:

## LIFE MARCHES ON

Hustle, bustle, scurry and worry—
Stop the world! I want to get off in a hurry,
But life marches on.

So much to do, so little time,
Deadlines to meet, and paths to climb,
But life marches on.

Babies so cuddly, so sweet and cute,
Then suddenly grown and off on their own.
Life marches on.

I look in the mirror, amazed at what I see!
What happened to my youth? Where is me?
Life marches on.

They say wisdom comes with age; I'm sure that's true,
But what good is all that wisdom when the memory
    is through?
Life marches on, and on, and on.

On a lighter note, there is another perk in Proverbs, the book of wisdom, but it is conditional:

The silver-haired head is a crown of glory, *If* it is found in the way of righteousness.
—PROVERBS 16:32, EMPHASIS ADDED

Let's get back to the theme of crowns as listed in the New Testament, taking them in the order of their appearance in scripture. There are five: (1) crown imperishable, (2) crown of righteousness, (3) crown of rejoicing, (4) crown of life, and (5) crown of glory.

**First is the crown imperishable**, as described in 1 Corinthians 9:

You've all been to the stadium and seen the athletes race. Everyone runs; one wins. Run to win. All good athletes train hard. They do it for a gold medal that tarnishes and fades. You're after one that's gold eternally. I don't know about you, but I'm running hard for the finish line. I'm giving it everything I've got. No sloppy living for me! I'm staying alert and in top

condition. I'm not going to get caught napping, telling everyone else all about it and then missing out myself.
—1 CORINTHIANS 9:24–27, THE MESSAGE

Paul was comparing our spiritual lives to an athletic event. In his day it would have been the Greek Olympic Games, where the crown would be made of wild olive branches, which would eventually wither and die. In modern times athletes seek the gold medal (first prize) in the Olympics, but these medals can tarnish and the glory fade away. All the athletes must train for the race, many for years; you cannot just decide today that you will run in the Olympics tomorrow. Top condition is required, and you must run with confidence because it is not a race for the faint-hearted. We are called to "lay aside every weight, and the sin which so easily ensnares us, and…run with endurance the race that is set before us, looking unto Jesus" (Heb. 12:1–2). We cannot just "talk the talk," and then miss out ourselves. We cannot possibly win if we are not in the race; we must enter the race and run to win the imperishable crown. No napping!

**Second is the crown of rejoicing** as described in 1 Thessalonians 2:19–20: this is the soul winner's crown. Paul is writing to the Thessalonian believers, asking two questions in verse 19 and giving the answer in verse 20 (the last sentence):

> For what is our hope, or joy, or crown of rejoicing? Is it not even you in the presence of our Lord Jesus Christ at His coming? For you are our glory and joy.

These new believers were Paul's "glory and joy." He was excited that upon the return of Jesus they would be a part of this family of God.

The greatest privilege and joy we have as Christians is to lead another person into a relationship with the Lord Jesus Christ. It is the great commission—not the great suggestion! Jesus said in Matthew 28:

> God authorized and commanded me to commission you: Go out and train everyone you meet, far and near, in this way of life, marking them by baptism in the threefold name: Father, Son, and Holy Spirit. Then instruct them in the practice of all I have commanded you. I'll be with you as you do this, day after day after day, right up to the end of the age.
> —MATTHEW 28:18–20, THE MESSAGE

This is a "way of life" and it is "day after day after day" until this age ends.

It is interesting to note that Cornelius, a centurion of the Italian Regiment, was called a devout man who gave alms and prayed to God always. In a vision the angel of God told him to send for Simon Peter to tell him what he must do (see Acts 10:1–6). Why could not that angel of God explain to Cornelius the good news of salvation? Answer: That is not the work of angels; that is the work of Christ's disciples—the ones who know from personal experience, fellow human beings who have been there and done that. Peter knew exactly what to say to Cornelius, and as you conclude reading Acts 10, you find that not only Cornelius but his entire household was saved, baptized, and filled with the Holy Spirit. But there was more! The Lord extended Peter's borders; he saw for himself and testified to the leaders at Jerusalem: "Then God has also granted to the Gentiles repentance to life" (Acts 11:18). Watch out, world—here we come!

I have been privileged to go on missions in many

countries where I have seen the Lord do mighty works of healing and deliverance, but the highest high is witnessing another person being "born again." Jesus told Nicodemus, "Most assuredly, I say to you, unless one is born again, he cannot see the kingdom of God" (John 3:3). It is the greatest miracle of all, because that person has been delivered from the kingdom of darkness and translated into the kingdom of light—hell lost and heaven gained.

Every conversion is sweet, but a few months ago I was part of one that went beyond. A dear friend's wife had left him, and he was devastated and distraught. This wife was dear to me as well. I suggested that he get back into church fellowship and talk with his pastor. He went on to share with me how active his parents had been and he knew his father especially to be a fine Christian, even a deacon in the church. Then I asked, "What about you?" He thought for a moment, and then acknowledged that he had never accepted Christ for himself. I shared some verses with him, and he invited Jesus to come into his heart. He knew he had to let go and let God work in his life and in his marriage. He made an appointment to meet with the pastor after church the following Sunday. The Lord, however, moved quickly; his wife returned and they went to church together that Sunday.

James 5:20 says that when we turn a sinner "from the error of his way," we "save a soul from death." Proverbs 11:30 says that "he who wins souls is wise." We also make heaven happy. Jesus said, "Likewise I say to you, there is joy in the presence of the angels of God over one sinner who repents" (Luke 15:10).

Jesus further said in Matthew 18:11–14:

> For the Son of Man has come to save that which was lost. What do you think? If a man has a hundred sheep, and one of them goes astray, does he not leave the ninety-nine and go to the mountains to seek the one that is straying? And if he should find it, assuredly, I say to you, he rejoices more over that sheep than over the ninety-nine that did not go astray. Even so it is not the will of your Father who is in heaven that one of these little ones should perish.

It is our Father's heart that none of His children should be lost, and Jesus came to carry out His plan—to have a family and that family be complete. As parents we can identify with the desire of our heavenly Father to have all His children safely in the fold. As members of the family of God, we want all our brothers and sisters to be saved—that none should perish.

You don't have to be a certain age, or be a Christian for a certain number of years, or have a college degree, or possess any other qualifications to be a soul winner. Love is the basic requirement. For instance, I have some missionary friends who are serving the Lord in Uganda. This couple has four small children. They decided they wanted to have a Bible club and invite the neighborhood children, most of whom did not know Jesus. There were approximately nineteen who attended. At the conclusion of the Bible club meeting, almost all of them did know Jesus. The few who did not left wanting to know more about this Jesus.

A young boy wanted desperately for his grandfather to accept Christ, and he repeatedly invited him to go to church. At last the grandfather consented, but to the dismay of the young boy, the preacher talked about all the "begats." He was so disappointed. When, if ever, would his grandfather come back to church because it had been so boring?

But surprise—when the altar call was given, his grandfather went forward! The boy asked what had prompted his response, and the grandfather said that all the "begats" made him aware of his own mortality.

We have God's promise that our labor will not be in vain in the Lord (see 1 Corinthians 15:58). The soul winner will not rejoice alone; all of heaven will celebrate with us when we receive the crown of rejoicing.

**Third is the crown of righteousness** as described in 2 Timothy 4:5–8:

> But you be watchful in all things, endure afflictions, do the work of an evangelist, fulfill your ministry. For I am already being poured out as a drink offering, and the time of my departure is at hand. I have fought the good fight, I have finished the race, I have kept the faith. Finally, there is laid up for me the crown of righteousness, which the Lord, the righteous Judge, will give to me on that Day, and not to me only but also to all who have loved His appearing.

When we receive Christ, we "become the righteousness of God in Him" (2 Cor. 5:21); this righteousness is imputed to all by His grace and through our faith. Noah "became heir of the righteousness which is according to faith" (Heb. 11:7). Paul speaks of this righteousness in his letter to the Romans, using Abraham as an example:

> He [Abraham] did not waver at the promise of God through unbelief, but was strengthened in faith, giving glory to God, and being fully convinced that what He had promised He was also able to perform. And therefore "it was accounted to him for righteousness." Now it was not written for his sake alone that it was imputed to him, but also for us. It shall

> be imputed to us who believe in Him who raised up
> Jesus our Lord from the dead, who was delivered up
> because of our offenses, and was raised because of
> our justification.
>
> —ROMANS 4:20–25

This imputed righteousness is part of our inheritance as believers. However, the crown of righteousness is a reward that we can earn by looking forward to and loving His second coming.

My dear friend is ninety-eight and presently resides in a nursing home where she witnesses to others at every opportunity. Her goal is to live until Jesus comes for His church in the Rapture. She has had many close calls, but each time she endures. I told her the Lord would have to sneak up on her during the night and hit her with a 2 x 4 so she would have no time to resist. Her love for Jesus and excitement about His return continues to influence her life. She taught Sunday school until almost ninety, and many in her class became preachers. Some other friends and I meet with her the first Thursday of each month, and she continues to color our lives. She has led us to many good "watering holes" where we have heard dynamic teaching. With her last breath, she will be witnessing for Jesus.

Paul's life was dynamically impacted by his belief in Christ's return. Note that as he was about to depart the earth, he could say, "I have fought the good fight, I have finished the race, I have kept the faith" (2 Tim. 4:7). He was able to look forward to the "judgment seat of Christ" (2 Cor. 5:10) because he knew the crown of righteousness was his to claim.

Jesus also is saying that the time is near: "Behold, I am coming quickly! Blessed is he who keeps the words of the prophecy of this book" (Rev. 22:7). Note the reply: "And the

Spirit and the bride say 'Come!'" (v. 17). The crown of righteousness awaits.

**Fourth is the crown of life** as described in James 1:12:

> Blessed is the man who endures temptation; for when he has been approved, he will receive the crown of life which the Lord has promised to those who love Him.

Jesus goes into more detail in His letter to the persecuted church in Smyrna in Revelation 2:10:

> Do not fear any of those things which you are about to suffer. Indeed, the devil is about to throw some of you into prison, that you may be tested, and you will have tribulation ten days. Be faithful until death, and I will give you the crown of life.

There is a difference between eternal life and the crown of life. All believers have eternal life (see John 3:15); however, not all believers will receive the crown of life. It is for those who are "faithful until death" (Rev. 2:10).

Jesus said in Matthew 10:38–39:

> And he who does not take his cross and follow after Me is not worthy of Me. He who finds his life will lose it, and he who loses his life for My sake will find it.

We can check the "Hall of Faith" in Hebrews 11 and find a roster of saints who died to self and lived for Christ. Certainly the apostles would be included, along with Paul. We could not begin to count the number of missionaries who have, and are now, sacrificing their lives for the sake of the gospel. The church is being persecuted today all over the world at an intensity that is astounding.

At this present time, Pastor Saeed Abedini, has been sentenced to eight years in Evin Prison in Iran. The Prayer Force in our church, consisting of eight dedicated women, has been praying since we first learned of his incarceration. We were delighted to receive an e-mail on May 15, 2013, from the International Leadership Institute requesting special prayer; it was encouraging to know that others were praying. Saeed refuses to recant his faith despite numerous beatings. He had been released from solitary confinement, where he had spent nine days, and Naghmeh, his wife, sent the following message:

> Saeed's family got to visit him at Evin Prison today since he has been released from solitary confinement. He said He felt many praying and the time in solitary was a time of intimacy with God. He said when he came out, the other prisoners said he was glowing! He was filled with more joy and peace after solitary than going in! All the prisoners were shocked at the change! This is because of your prayers.

The e-mail continued:

> Please continue to pray for Saeed's health. Pray he will be healed of his internal bleeding.

Thousands have signed a petition addressed to the president of Iran requesting his release. At a meeting of the United Nations in New York City in September 2013, Saeed's wife was staying at the same hotel as the Iranian delegation. She was able to deliver a letter Saeed had smuggled out of prison to a member of the delegation, and she saw him open the letter and read it. Later there was a report that President Obama had spoken with the Iranian president and asked that Saeed be released. Billy Graham has also personally written a letter and Secretary of State Kerry has formally addressed the issue. I pray when you read this chapter, dear reader, this will be old news and Pastor Saeed will be free. This courageous young man surely has the crown of life awaiting him; he has put his life on the line and is enduring trials, testings and temptations in the power of the love of God.

> When Moses came down from Mount Sinai with the two tablets of the covenant law in his hands, he was not aware that his face was radiant because he had spoken with the LORD.
> —EXODUS 34:29, NIV

**Fifth is the crown of glory** as described in 1 Peter 5:2–4:

> Shepherd the flock of God which is among you, serving as overseers, not by compulsion but willingly, not for dishonest gain but eagerly; or as being lords over those entrusted to you, but being examples to the flock; and when the Chief Shepherd appears, you will receive the crown of glory that does not fade away.

This is a special crown reserved for faithful, obedient pastors. The Chief Shepherd will bestow upon them this eternal reward. Not all believers are called to be pastors over flocks, so is this an "exclusive" crown? There is a promise for all believers in Matthew 10:41:

> He who receives a prophet in the name of a prophet shall receive a prophet's reward. And he who receives

a righteous man in the name of a righteous man
shall receive a righteous man's reward.

When I joined Powder Springs First United Methodist
Church, I made a vow to uphold the church with my prayers,
my presence, my tithes, and my offerings. The pastor is the
overseer, the shepherd of our church; so when I pray for my
pastor and the congregation, attend worship services and
growth classes, and support the church through my tithes
and offerings (money, talents, and time), then I am supporting my pastor's ministry. I am encouraging my pastor
in the work of the Lord; hence, I am making an invest-
ment in this righteous man and I likewise earn a crown of
glory. My motive in supporting my pastor and my church,
of course, cannot be to earn a crown but to be obedient to
the cause of Christ. He came to establish the church; He is
"head of the church" and the "church is subject to Christ,"
and "Christ also loved the church and gave Himself for her"
(Eph. 5:23–25). We are warned not to forsake "the assembling of ourselves together" (Heb. 10:25). If my Lord loved
the church enough to die for her, surely I can love my Lord
enough to live for her.

The pastor will earn this crown of glory for himself by
feeding the flock. Timothy's instructions are to "Preach
the Word! Be ready in season and out of season. Convince,
rebuke, exhort, with all longsuffering and teaching" (2 Tim.
4:2). He is to take charge of the spiritual oversight of the
church; He is the shepherd and the flock has been com-
mitted to his care and keeping. He is to be an example
to the flock. The congregation can safely and confidently
follow him because he is following Jesus, and the pastor can
rest assured that he has their support. There is unity, which
brings blessing. David wrote in Psalm 133:1–3:

> Behold, how good and how pleasant it is For brethren
> to dwell together in unity! It is like the precious oil
> upon the head, Running down on the beard, The
> beard of Aaron, Running down on the edge of his
> garments. It is like the dew of Hermon, Descending
> upon the mountains of Zion; For there the LORD
> commanded the blessing—Life forevermore.

Once again, our Lord goes exceedingly above and beyond,
for along with the crown of glory there is the blessing.

These are the five crowns that are laid up for the followers of Christ, but we would be remiss if we failed to consider another crown, the crown of thorns.

> So then Pilate took Jesus and scourged Him. And the
> soldiers twisted a crown of thorns and put it on His
> head, and they put on Him a purple robe. Then they
> said, "Hail, King of the Jews!" And they struck Him
> with their hands. Pilate then went out again and said
> to them, "Behold, I am bringing Him out to you, that
> you may know that I find no fault in Him." Then Jesus
> came out, wearing the crown of thorns and the purple
> robe. And Pilate said to them, "Behold the Man!"
> —JOHN 19:1–5

The scourging by the soldiers and the subsequent beating
fulfilled the prophecy of Isaiah 50:6:

> I gave My back to those who struck Me, And My
> cheeks to those who plucked out the beard; I did not
> hide my face from shame and spitting.

Pilate certainly could "find no fault in Him," because
Jesus was without sin. However, the Father "made Him who
knew no sin to be sin for us, that we might become the

righteousness of God in Him" (2 Cor. 5:21). Pilate correctly referred to Jesus as the "Man." Jesus referred to Himself often as the "Son of Man." All of His divinity was contained in a human body because He came to die on the cross to atone for our sins—to pay for our "at-one-ment" with God. He was our Passover Lamb.

It was proper that the crown He wore that day was of thorns, because thorns were symbolic of the curse that came when Adam and Eve sinned in the Garden of Eden by their disobedience. It is recorded in Genesis 3:17–19:

> Cursed is the ground for your sake; In toil you shall eat of it All the days of your life. Both thorns and thistles it shall bring forth for you, And you shall eat the herb of the field. In the sweat of your face you shall eat bread Till you return to the ground, For out of it you were taken; For dust you are And to dust you shall return.

Jesus bore the crown of thorns and He sweat drops of blood for us in another garden—the Garden of Gethsemane.

But that is not the end of the story. In Revelation 19:11–16 there is another exciting account of Christ, and He returns on a white horse, our conquering hero:

> Now I saw heaven opened, and behold, a white horse. And He who sat on him was called Faithful and True, and in righteousness He judges and makes war. His eyes were like a flame of fire, and on His head were many crowns. He had a name written that no one knew except Himself. He was clothed with a robe dipped in blood, and His name is called The Word of God. And the armies in heaven, clothed in fine linen, white and clean, followed Him on white horses. Now

out of His mouth goes a sharp sword, that with it He should strike the nations. And He Himself will rule them with a rod of iron. He Himself treads the winepress of the fierceness and wrath of Almighty God. And He has on His robe and on His thigh a name written: KING OF KINGS AND LORD OF LORDS.

## WONDER OF WONDERS

Wonder of wonders, how can it be—
That Jesus, my Lord, came to earth for me!

Wonder of wonders, how can it be—
That Jesus, my Lord, gave His life for me!

Wonder of wonders, how can it be—
That Jesus, my Lord, died on Calvary.
He broke death's grip to give me a heavenly trip!
Wonder of wonders, how can it be?

Wonder of wonders, how can it be—
That Jesus, my Lord, is coming for me!
We have a date for all of eternity!
Wonder of wonders, how can it be?

Wonder of wonders, how can it be—
That Jesus, my Lord, left Glory for me,
To be born in a manger in Bethlehem,
Where God placed in the hay His Precious Gem.

Wonder of wonders, how can it be—
That Jesus, my Lord, did all this for me!

## Chapter 8
# IRRI-TATER

**W**EBSTER'S DEFINES IRRITATE as the following:

To provoke, annoy, cause impatience or anger; to produce irritation in; to stimulate to action, said of a muscle, contracted by artificial stimulation. Syn. aggravate, excite, worry, provoke, embitter, exasperate, madden, fret, inflame, tease, anger, vex, pique, nettle, incense. Ant. Comfort, soothe.

I grew up with a sister who was four years younger than I, and I would be a millionaire today if I had a dime for every time I was told, "Don't aggravate your sister!" What about the times she "irritated/provoked/teased/aggravated" me? It's her fault I have a chipped front bottom tooth!

This coin of irritation has two sides because irritation can be positive as well as negative. Isn't a pearl the result of an oyster being irritated by a grain of sand? In the Book of Revelation there is a description of the New Jerusalem, having "a great and high wall with twelve gates" (Rev. 21:12). There is more detail in verse 21: "The twelve gates were twelve pearls: each individual gate was of one pearl." Does this not suggest that the citizens of the kingdom of heaven do not enter lightly into the city? The sufferings, trials and tribulations of the saints have produced pearls.

Jean Paul Richter says: "The burden of suffering seems a tombstone hung about our necks, while in reality it is only the weight which is necessary to keep down the diver while he is hunting for pearls."[1]

Jesus told this parable about the kingdom of heaven:

> Again, the kingdom of heaven is like a merchant seeking beautiful pearls, who, when he had found one pearl of great price, went and sold all that he had and bought it.
>
> —MATTHEW 13:45–46

In this teaching we see that the merchant is our Lord Jesus Christ; He has found one pearl of exquisite beauty. Every born-again child of God represents a valuable pearl, but together we make up the church, the bride of Christ. We are one in "the unity of the Spirit...one body and one Spirit" (Eph. 4:3–4). Jesus gave all He had—His very life—to pay the high cost of our sin. Consider all the irritation our Lord endured to provoke the change in our lives—to translate us from the kingdom of darkness into the kingdom of light.

It's how we respond to the irritation that makes the difference. Sometimes we may be called to be an irritator to accomplish change that is beneficial. On the other hand, the enemy is adept at sending irritators into our lives to steal our peace, to cause us to worry, to become bitter and angry—you get the picture.

The Book of Nehemiah is a vivid illustration of good irritators versus bad irritators. During the Babylonian exile, Nehemiah served King Artaxerxes as his cup bearer, and it was part of his job to be a "happy camper." If he did not have a happy face before the king, it could cost him his head! Nehemiah had received distressing news that the wall of Jerusalem was broken down and its gates burned with fire, leaving the people defenseless (Neh. 1:3). Nehemiah had prayed, asking God to give him the king's favor (v. 11); Nehemiah was irritated and provoked to action.

As Nehemiah gave wine to the king, the king discerned Nehemiah's "sorrow of heart" and asked the cause (Neh. 2:2). When Nehemiah explained the state of affairs in Jerusalem, the king granted his request to return to Jerusalem and rebuild the wall and further provided a military escort, the necessary letters to the various governors for permits, and building materials. (See Nehemiah 2:3–9.)

Now "bad irritators" enter the scene in verse 10:

> When Sanballat the Horonite and Tobiah the Ammonite official heard of it, they were deeply disturbed that a man had come to seek the well-being of the children of Israel.

Nehemiah conducted a secret survey of the broken walls and the burned gates. He then approached the priests, nobles, officials and the others who would be doing the work (vv. 11–16).

> Then I said to them, "You see the distress that we are in, how Jerusalem lies waste, and its gates are burned with fire. Come and let us build the wall of Jerusalem, that we may no longer be a reproach." And I told them of the hand of my God which had been good upon me, and also of the king's words that he had spoken to me. So they said, "Let us rise up and build." Then they set their hands to this good work.
> —NEHEMIAH 2:17–18

Nehemiah is provoking them to do a "good work." But the bad irritators are irritated. Sanballat and Tobiah are joined by Geshem the Arab, and they began to ridicule

Nehemiah and the workers (v. 19). However, Nehemiah is not to be deterred. As recorded in chapter 3, he delegates, assigning various sections of the walls and gates to certain teams, thus unifying the people. As progress was made, the bad irritators became more vocal and they conspired to attack Jerusalem and cause confusion (4:1–8.)

Nehemiah and the laborers "loaded themselves so that with one hand they worked at construction, and with the other held a weapon" (v. 17). While on a mission to Monterrey, Mexico, I heard a local pastor preach on this verse and it made an impression on me. He said that as we are about our task of building and advancing the kingdom of God, we must keep a brick in one hand and the sword in the other, that sword being the Word of God. The logo of an irritator for good could very well be a construction worker with a brick in one hand and a Bible in the other and with the helmet or hard hat of salvation on his head, gospel boots on his feet, and a big tool belt of truth around his waist.

As often is the case when we are completing a task assigned to us by the Lord, minor irritations arise for the purpose of distraction. The nobles and rulers had been abusing the people, charging them high rates of interest, forcing their children into slavery, and taking their land. Nehemiah called for a stop to this usury and for restoration, to which the lenders agreed (see chapter 5).

Sanballat, Tobiah, Geshem, and all the other bad irritators tried to pull Nehemiah away from his work, calling him to a meeting on the plain of Ono; but Nehemiah knew they were seeking to do him harm (6:2) and he replied:

> I am doing a great work, so that I cannot come *down*.
> Why should the work cease while I leave it and go
> *down* to you?
>
> —NEHEMIAH 6:3, EMPHASIS ADDED

Four times the message is sent, and four times Nehemiah declines the invitation (v. 4). Then Sanballat writes a letter accusing Nehemiah of plotting to become king, and a false prophet urges Nehemiah to meet in the temple in order to save his life (vv. 5–7). However, Nehemiah perceives that this is a trap and he refuses to go (vv. 8–13).

> So the wall was finished on the twenty-fifth day of
> Elul, in fifty-two days. And it happened, when all our
> enemies heard of it, and all the nations around us saw
> these things, that they were very disheartened [irri-
> tated] in their own eyes; for they perceived that this
> work was done by our God...Then it was, when the
> wall was built and I had hung the doors, when the
> gatekeepers, the singers, and the Levites had been
> appointed, that I gave the charge of Jerusalem to my
> brother Hanani, and Hananiah the leader of the cit-
> adel, for he was a faithful man and feared God more
> than many.
>
> —NEHEMIAH 6:15–16; 7:1–2

Edmund Burke said, "All that is necessary for the triumph of evil is that good men do nothing."[2] Nehemiah responded to God's call; therefore, evil did not triumph.

John Wesley encouraged good men (and women): "Do all the good you can. By all the means you can. In all the ways you can. In all the places you can. At all the times you can. To all the people you can. As long as ever you can."[3] Wouldn't that irritate the devil!

Jesus said that Satan, the thief, comes "to steal, and to

kill, and to destroy" (John 10:10). When we are bad irritators, we do the same to others. We steal their joy, kill their hope, and destroy their dreams. A friend of mine once said that there are in this world attic and basement people. The attic people pull you up, while the basement people pull you down. Many times when she calls, she will say, "Hello, Betty; this is Polly, your attic friend!" It's a delight to hear her voice; she always leaves me "high."

Others who call do not have to announce that they are basement people because their conversation gives them away. Every word is negative, spoken in the confident expectation of a dismal future. They are like the Hebrew children, complaining as they circled Mt. Sinai; and later when Moses sent out the twelve spies to give him a report on the Promised Land, ten brought back a bad report. Only Joshua and Caleb wanted to march in and take the land. The people, again with their negative words, had to spend forty more years in the wilderness. When the naysayers had died off, Joshua led the next generation to Jericho—the door to the Promised Land. But this time Joshua commanded the people:

> You shall not shout or make any noise with your voice, nor shall a word proceed out of our mouth, until the day I say to you, "Shout!" Then you shall shout.
> —JOSHUA 6:10

When the Lord gave the instructions to Joshua to march around the walls one time each for six days, he gave the order of procession. On the seventh day, they were to march seven times, and when the priests gave one long blast with the ram's horn, then they were to shout and the walls would fall down (Josh. 6:3–5). The Lord did not say they could not speak. Joshua added that command because of his past experience; he did not want them to talk themselves out of the promise. I expect he was a bit weary of the wilderness wandering; he was ready to get on with the show.

My mother used to tell me, "If you can't say anything good, then don't say anything at all." That is good advice today. I wonder how many times I've talked myself out of a promise or an achievement, something I could have accomplished if I had not listened to my negative self-talk. What about you, dear reader?

My son Scott accused me once of being rude to his friends when they called. He said I sounded like I was angry at them. That was not my intention, so I put a little red heart sticker on the telephone above the receiver; when I answered it would remind me to be loving and kind. A wise prayer is: "Set a guard, O LORD, over my mouth; Keep watch over the door of my lips...That I might not sin against You" (Ps. 141:3; 119:11).

The "E-Test" over our words should be: Do they encourage, edify, and exhort? If not, don't loose them into the universe, because our words are powerful. The old saying, "Sticks and stones may break my bones, but words will never hurt me," is a lie from the pit of hell. Words do hurt and they do break spirits.

In Genesis we read that God spoke and created our world: heavens, earth, constellations, animals, fish, and finally His masterpiece—man! Jesus spoke and miracles happened— the blind could see, the lame could walk, the deaf could hear, the sick were made well, the dead were raised to life, and best of all; man was redeemed from the curse of the law, and by calling on His name we are saved and adopted into the family of God. His Word, the Bible, is living and alive. David wrote in Psalm 107:20: "He sent His word and healed them, And delivered them from their destructions." There is a serious warning in Matthew 12:36–37:

> But I say to you that for every idle word men may speak, they will give account of it in the day of judgment. For by your words you will be justified, and by your words you will be condemned.

Looking at my life, I recall some of those good words that brought me joy unspeakable: I'm so proud of you; you are such a pretty little girl; you are so smart; you made the team; you have been promoted; you are hired; will you marry me; you have a son; you have a daughter; Mom, I met this girl/boy; this is not malignant; we want to publish your book; I'm sorry; forgive me; I love you.

Some bad ones were heart-breaking: you didn't make the team; we are not hiring now; the "rabbit test" was negative; I want a divorce; we don't have room for you; it is cancer; we have done all we can; they are gone.

Upon return from a mission to Zimbabwe, I received a request from a student who needed a certain book for a class he was taking; without the book he would fail. I went to a lot of trouble and expense to locate the book, have it delivered to me, and then forward to him. He never did thank me or even acknowledge receipt. I did find out later from another source that he had indeed received the book. His ingratitude made me very sad.

In 1 Thessalonians 5:18, Paul instructed the believers: "In everything give thanks; for this is the will of God in Christ Jesus for you." Note the preposition *in*. The word is not *for* everything, because many things that come to us are yucky; such as sickness, disease, death, accidents, loss, and the like.

But we know that our Father is in control; and as He goes with us through the "things," we come out like shining gold, more mature than when we entered the particular circumstance. The truth of the matter is that we do our most growing in the valleys; and when we arrive at last, the view from those mountaintops is awesome. It is God's will, in Christ Jesus, that we practice an attitude of gratitude.

When Jesus fed the five thousand with a lad's lunch, He gave us this example:

> And Jesus took the loaves, and when He had given thanks He distributed them to the disciples, and the disciples to those sitting down; and likewise of the fish, as much as they wanted. So when they were filled, He said to the disciples, "Gather up the fragments that remain, so that nothing is lost."
>
> —JOHN 6:11–12

Note that Jesus did not give to the disciples until He had thanked the Father, His Source. The disciples then gave to the people the loaves and fishes, which had been multiplied by thanksgiving.

> Someone has said, Thank God for the Starlight, and He will give you the Moonlight. Thank Him for the Moonlight, and He will give you the Sunlight. Thank Him for the Sunlight, and by and by He will take you where He Himself is the Light.[4]

Paul warned Timothy that "professional liars" would come on the scene:

> They'll tell you not to eat this or that food—perfectly good food God created to be eaten heartily and with thanksgiving by believers who know better!

Everything God created is good, and to be received
with thanks. Nothing is to be sneered at and thrown
out. God's Word and our prayers make every item in
creation holy.

—1 TIMOTHY 4:3–5, THE MESSAGE

I trained my children to say grace or the blessing before
meals; we would thank God for our food. I told them this
would make the food good for us, and we would not get a
bellyache.

The Bible tells of an occasion when Mary and Martha
sent for Jesus to come because their brother, Lazarus, was
sick. After two days Jesus went, but Lazarus had died, which
was a part of the plan because Jesus wanted the disciples to
"believe" (John 11:15) when He said in verses 25–26:

I am the resurrection and the life. He who believes
in Me, though he may die, he shall live. And whoever lives and believes in Me shall never die. Do you
believe this?

This was crucial to their faith because soon Jesus would
be crucified and they would be going through some dark
days pending His resurrection. They needed to deposit this
experience in their memory bank.

Jesus is taken to the tomb, and there He commands that
the stone be rolled away. Martha protests because "he has
been dead four days" (v. 39). Jesus reminds Martha that if
she only believes, she "would see the glory of God" (v. 40).
The stone is rolled away, and Jesus said,

"Father, I *thank* You that You have heard Me. And I
know that You always hear Me, but because of the
people who are standing by I said this, that they may
believe that You sent Me." Now when He had said

these things, He cried with a loud voice, "Lazarus, come forth!"

—JOHN 11:41–43, EMPHASIS ADDED

And he did! Jesus again shows us the importance of thanksgiving.

Followers of Christ celebrate Communion, the Lord's Supper. The Greek word for communion is *eucharist*, which means thanksgiving. We read this account in 1 Corinthians 11:23–26:

> The Lord Jesus on the same night in which He was betrayed took bread, and when He had given thanks, He broke it and said, "Take, eat, this is My body which is broken for you; do this in remembrance of Me." In the same manner He also took the cup after supper, saying, "This cup is the new covenant of My blood. This do, as often as you drink it, in remembrance of Me." For as often as you eat this bread and drink this cup, you proclaim The Lord's death till He comes.

Jesus, the Son of God, gave thanks to Father God, knowing that within hours He would be facing an agonizing death by crucifixion. But then, that is why He came—to pay the ultimate price for our sins by the shedding of His blood—and He was thankful.

Sarah Young has written a devotional book entitled *Jesus Calling* containing personal messages from God received as she meditated on Him. The entry for July 24 impacted my heart, and I pray it does the same for you, dear reader:

> Thankfulness opens the door to My Presence. Though I am always with you, I have gone to great measures to preserve your freedom of choice. I have placed a

door between you and Me, and I have empowered you to open or close that door. There are many ways to open it, but a grateful attitude is one of the most effective. Thankfulness is built on a substructure of trust. When thankful words stick in your throat, you need to check up on your foundation of trust. When thankfulness flows freely from your heart and lips, let your gratitude draw you closer to me. I want you to learn the art of GIVING THANKS IN ALL CIRCUMSTANCES. See how many times you can thank Me daily; this will awaken your awareness to a multitude of blessings. It will also cushion the impact of trials when they come against you. Practice My presence by practicing the discipline of thankfulness.[5]

Carrying this further, how does our Lord feel when we are not thankful for all He does for us every day—for our very lives, the air we breathe, food we eat, good health, families, friends, prosperity, freedom, butterflies, chocolate? The list is endless; and most of all, our names in the Lamb's Book of Life. Why would we, through an attitude of ingratitude, hurt the feelings of the One we love and the One who loves us most?

## THANK YOU

"Thank you" is a powerful phrase,
When spoken aloud it causes hearts to raise;
But when these words are withheld,
Spirits are broken and hearts are felled.

We enter our Lord's gates with thanksgiving—
An attitude of gratitude is our guide for life.
In every situation Jesus gave thanks to the Father;
We were shown the way by our Elder Brother.

So we say, "Thank You, Father, for the gift of Your
    Son,
And pray for His soon return—Your Kingdom to
    come.
Mold us, Holy Spirit, into instruments of love,
Filled with Living Water from Your storehouse
    above."

Thank You, Father!
Thank You, Son!
Thank You, Holy Spirit!
The Godhead—Three in One.

# Chapter 9
# IMI-TATER

**W**EBSTER'S DEFINES IMITATE this way: "To produce a likeness of, as to imitate another person's mannerisms; to take as a model; copy, mimic; to resemble." Jesus was teaching the disciples about the Father, and He said:

> "If you had known Me, you would have known My Father also; and from now on you know Him and have seen Him." Philip said to Him, "Lord, show us the Father, and it is sufficient for us." Jesus said to him, "Have I been with you so long, and yet you have not known Me, Philip? He who has seen Me has seen the Father; so how can you say, 'show us the Father?' Do you not believe that I am in the Father, and the Father in Me? The words that I speak to you, I do not speak on My own authority; but the Father who dwells in Me does the works."
> —JOHN 14:7–10

Jesus is in essence saying that He is "God the Father with skin on!" Does it thus follow that Christians ideally are "Jesus with skin on?"

Paul writes about a mystery to the church at Colossae:

> I now rejoice in my sufferings for you, and fill up in my flesh what is lacking in the afflictions of Christ, for the sake of His body, which is the church, of

which I became a minister according to the stewardship from God which was given to me for you, to fulfill the word of God, the mystery which has been hidden from ages and from generations, but now has been revealed to His saints. To them God willed to make known what are the riches of the glory of this mystery among the Gentiles: which is Christ in you, the hope of glory.

—COLOSSIANS 1:24–27

Question: Who is "the hope of glory?" Is it Christ or is it the saints, the followers of Christ?

In the Book of John 3:17–18 we read:

For God did not send His Son into the world to condemn the world, but that the world through Him might be saved. He who believes in Him is not condemned; but he who does not believe is condemned already, because he has not believed in the name of the only begotten Son of God.

Continuing in John 14:6:

Jesus said to him, "I am the way, the truth, and the life. No one comes to the Father except through Me."

Only through Christ and His sacrifice can we be saved. Accordingly, He is our hope of glory. However, in Paul's first letter, written approximately twenty years after the resurrection, he writes to the church of the Thessalonians:

For what is our hope, or joy, or crown of rejoicing? Is it not even you in the presence of our Lord Jesus Christ at His coming? For you are our glory and joy.

—1 THESSALONIANS 2:19–20

Paul is telling the Thessalonian converts that they are his hope and glory, and he exhorts them "in the Lord Jesus Christ that you should abound more and more" (4:1). They were to add to the kingdom, like a tag team. Jesus had tagged His followers, charging them with the Great "Co-Mission" in Mark 16:15: "Go into all the world and preach the gospel to every creature." Jesus subsequently manifested Himself to Paul, and then Paul was charged to go and re-present Jesus to his world. Jesus is still calling His disciples today to go and tell.

Jesus prayed for *all* believers (past, present, and future) in His priestly prayer preceding His arrest and subsequent crucifixion:

> I do not pray for these alone, but also for those who will believe in Me through their word [Christians]; that they all may be one, as You, Father, are in Me, and I in You; that they also may be one in Us, that the world may believe that You sent Me. And the glory which You gave Me, I have given them, that they may be one just as We are one: I in them, and You in Me; that they may be made perfect in one, and that the world may know that You have sent Me, and have loved them as You have loved Me. Father, I desire that they also whom You gave Me may be with Me where I am, that they may behold My glory which You gave Me before the foundation of the world. O righteous Father! The world has not known You, but I have known You; and these have known that You sent Me. And I have declared to them Your name, and will declare it, that the love with which You loved Me may be in them, and I in them.
> —JOHN 17:20–26

Jesus wants to share His glory with all His followers. His desire is for them to be with the Father and with Him, experiencing this love the Father has for His Son and the love the Son has for the Father and the family (the church) which the Father has given the Son. This body of Christ, the church, is His bride—His hope of glory. In turn, our Lord Jesus Christ is the church's hope of glory. It is a circle of love.

Going back to Paul's letter to his first congregation, the Thessalonians, he says in 1 Thessalonians 1:3:

> Remembering without ceasing your work of faith, and labor of love, and patience in hope in our Lord Jesus Christ, in the sight of God and our Father.

Paul is very proud of this church. Compare these words to the letter Jesus wrote to the church of Ephesus:

> I know your works, your labor, your patience... Nevertheless, I have this against you, that you have left your first love.
> —REVELATION 2:2, 4

Note that the Thessalonians had "work[s] of faith, and labor of love, and patience in hope." The Ephesians had only works (no faith), labor (no love) and patience (no hope); they had left their "first love." In the love chapter (1 Cor. 13:13), we are told that there "now abide faith, hope, love, these three; but the greatest of these is love."

A friend shared with me that he had lost his first love. I was so sad; and since he was divorced, I assumed he meant his former wife. He countered, "Oh, no! I don't mean my wife; I mean Jesus!" That made me even sadder.

If you lose something, you go back to where you last had

it. What happened to cause this loss? In a relationship with Jesus, what has intervened to cut the cord? In any relationship there must be communication. Are you praying daily and consistently (without ceasing)? Are you getting the Word into you, such as Word-based books but especially by reading the Bible? Are you meditating on the Word, chewing on it like a cow chews on its cud?

What about church? We are not to forsake the assembling of ourselves together (Heb. 10:25). "So then faith comes by hearing, and hearing by the Word of God" (Rom. 10:17). We need to hear the Word preached, read, sung, and spoken. Listen to the testimonies of the saints; rehearse your testimony. Word in = faith out.

What about the Holy Spirit? There is that initial infilling that Jesus talked about more fully prior to His ascension (Acts 1:4–8), and the outpouring in the Upper Room on the Day of Pentecost (Acts 2:1–4). The Holy Spirit empowers us to be witnesses for Jesus, to become all He has planned for us to be. His primary assignment is to reveal the reality of Jesus; He is a Pointer to Jesus. He has even been referred to as the Hound of Heaven. We are to be filled and continuously filled with the Holy Spirit (Eph. 5:18). If your love tank is running on low, run to Jesus, the Baptizer, and ask for a fresh filling. If we just A-ask, S-seek, and K-knock, the Holy Spirit will gladly come in His fullness. After all, He's the one who led you to Jesus in the first place, and He comes to be your Helper.

You must be a clean vessel, because the Spirit is Holy; get rid of those sins that so easily clog your pipes. One of the main "cloggers" is unforgiveness. Forgiveness is not an option with a Christian. Christ forgave from the cross when He prayed: "Father, forgive them, for they do not know what they do" (Luke 23:34). When we pray the Lord's

Prayer: "And forgive us our debts, as we forgive our debtors" (Matt. 6:12), we make our forgiveness conditional upon our forgiving others. Jesus put it bluntly:

> For if you forgive men their trespasses, your heavenly Father will also forgive you. But if you do not forgive men their trespasses, neither will your Father forgive your trespasses.
>
> —MATTHEW 6:14–15

We know we are to forgive the "big" offenses, but those little one can be sneaky. We slowly pile up the nickel and dime stuff, and then one day we find that our pipe is clogged and the Holy Spirit is not able to flow through us. As followers of Christ and His commandments, we are not to "keep score of the sins of others" (1 Cor. 13:5, THE MESSAGE).

Love is the most powerful force in all of the universe, "for God is Love," and we are called to love also:

> He who does not love does not know God, for God is love In this the love of God was manifested toward us, that God has sent His only begotten Son into the world, that we might live through Him. In this is love, not that we loved God, but that He loved us and sent His Son to be the propitiation for our sins. Beloved, if God so loved us, we also ought to love one another.
>
> —1 JOHN 4:8–11

Paul writes to the church at Ephesus:

> Therefore be imitators of God as dear children. And walk in love, as Christ also has loved us and given Himself for us, an offering and a sacrifice to God for a sweet-smelling aroma…For you were once darkness, but now you are light in the Lord. Walk

as children of light (for the fruit of the Spirit is in all goodness, righteousness, and truth), finding out what is acceptable to the Lord. And have no fellowship with the unfruitful works of darkness, but rather expose them…See then that you walk circumspectly, not as fools but as wise, redeeming the time, because the days are evil. Therefore do not be unwise, but understanding what the will of the Lord is. And do not be drunk with wine, in which is dissipation; but be filled with the Spirit.

—EPHESIANS 5:1–2, 8–11, 15–18

Jesus gave us the eleventh commandment in John 13:34–35:

A new commandment I give to you, that you love one another; as I have loved you, that you also love one another. By this all will know that you are My disciples, if you have love for one another.

Charles Caleb Colton said: "Imitation is the sincerest form of flattery."[1] When we imitate Christ we walk in love, in light, in wisdom, and in the Spirit. Others will see Jesus in us and be drawn by the fruit of the Holy Spirit in us, which is "love, joy, peace, longsuffering, kindness, goodness, faithfulness, gentleness, self-control" (Gal. 5:22–23). That last verse continues: "Against such [all this good stuff] there is no law." We won't beat our brothers and sisters over the head with the law, but we will love them into the kingdom through grace.

My son Steve was working in the basement one day and his little boy Ryan was with him. Steve took a screwdriver to tighten a screw on his kayak. Ryan copied Steve, pretending to tighten a screw even though he was too little to know what he was doing. Steve had one of those epiphanies, an "ah-hah" moment: "My son is going to be watching my life, imitating me." He was struck with the awesome responsibility of being a good father for the good of his son.

On another occasion, many years later, my son Steve was driving his family, including me, home from a vacation in Panama Beach, Florida. I was asking his advice on some matters; and as he answered, it occurred to me that our roles had somehow reversed—he was more like the parent than I; he was taking care of me and he was in the driver's seat.

## When Did You Pass Me?

It seems like only yesterday—
I was the Mom and you were my little boy.
I was the one who wiped your tears away.
Your first steps and first words brought such joy!

I took you to school on that very first day;
I should have seen the change coming right away.
The time so quickly passed—suddenly it was the
       last—
You left home and started your own nest.

Now I sit in the back seat, with my grandchildren.
You, my son, are driving me; I call on you for
       wisdom.
Time slipped by and I got old, leaving this question
       that nags my soul:
When did you pass me?
I must have been asleep!

# Chapter 10
## SWEET-TATER

**W**HEN I WAS a young girl, my mom occasionally would let me go over to a friend's house to play or perhaps even spend the night. Her last words always were: "You be sweet now, you hear?" She did not have to define *sweet* to me; I knew she meant to be pleasant, gentle, kind, and well-mannered—all the charming things. I was not to bring shame on my family.

Is it any wonder that we call those we especially love our "sweethearts?" Did you ever take a pen and draw a heart in the palm of your hand, with a cross in the middle and your initials on each side of the top line and your sweetheart's initials on each side of the bottom? Mine was B. T. + B. S. That meant Betty Terry loves Bob Smith. But it gets better because our Lord says: "See, I have inscribed you in the palms of My Hands" (Isa. 49:16). We are His sweethearts! That is really sweet.

King David wrote: "How sweet are Your words to my taste, sweeter than honey to my mouth" (Ps. 119:103). Psalm 119 is the longest chapter in the Bible, containing 176 verses. Its caption in my New King James Version of *The Christian Life Bible* is "Meditations on the Excellencies of the Word of God."[1]

My mother had been calling me to excellence when she instructed me to be sweet. However, there is more to these sweet words that David was speaking about in Psalm 119:103. There is power, as set forth in Psalm 33:6–7:

> By the word of the LORD the heavens were made, And all the host of them by the breath of His mouth. He gathers the waters of the sea together as a heap; He lays up the deep in storehouses.

God uses creation to show Himself to the world, tangible evidence of His reality. In Romans 1:18–20 there is a dire warning:

> For the wrath of God is revealed from heaven against all ungodliness and unrighteousness of men, who suppress the truth in unrighteousness, because what may be known of God is manifest in them, for God has showed it to them. For since the creation of the world His invisible attributes are clearly seen, being understood by the things that are made, even His eternal power and Godhead, so that they are without excuse.

Of course, man himself is God's most excellent work, His crowning achievement, for we are made in His image (Gen. 1:26). In the Genesis account of creation, we read that at the end of each day's work, the Lord announced that "it was good" (Gen. 1:4, 10, 12, 18, 21, 25), but in verses 26–28, we read:

> Then God said, "Let us make man in Our image, according to Our likeness; let them have dominion over the fish of the sea, over the birds of the air, and over the cattle, over all the earth, and over every creeping thing that creeps on the earth." So God

made man in His own image; in the image of God He created them. Then God blessed them.

And in verse 31:

Then God saw everything that He had made, and indeed it was very good.

Getting back to excellence, Psalm 8:1, 3–6, 9:

O Lord, our Lord, How excellent is Your name in all the earth, Who have set Your glory above the heavens!…When I consider Your heavens, the work of Your fingers, The moon and the stars, which You have ordained, What is man that You are mindful of him, And the son of man that You visit him? For you have made him a little lower than the angels, And have crowned him with glory and honor. You have made him to have dominion over the works of Your hands, You have put all things under his feet…O Lord, our Lord, how excellent is Your name in all the earth!

It gets better even than this! Our heavenly Father, as an ultimate act of sweetness, kindness, mercy, and grace, sent His Son. Just in case we didn't "get it," John spells it out for us:

In the beginning was the Word, and the Word was with God, and the Word was God. He was in the beginning with God. All things were made through Him, and without Him nothing was made that was made. In Him was life, and the life was the light of men. And the light shines in the darkness and the darkness did not comprehend it…That was the true Light, which gives light to every man coming into the world. He was in the world, and the world was made through Him, and the world did not know Him. He came to His own, and His own did not receive Him. But as many as received Him, to them He gave the right to become children of God, to those who believe in His name: who were born, not of blood, nor of the will of the flesh, nor of the will of man, but of God. And the Word became flesh and dwelt among us, and we beheld His Glory, the glory as of the only begotten of the Father, full of grace and truth...And of His fullness we have all received, and grace for grace. For the law was given through Moses, but grace and truth came through Jesus Christ. No one has seen God at any time. The only begotten Son, who is in the bosom of the Father, He has declared Him.

—JOHN 1:1–5, 9–14, 16–18

I wrote this notation in my Bible many years ago; I do not know the source, but it touched my heart: "Jesus is who man thinks of when he thinks of God; Jesus is who God thinks of when He thinks of man." Jesus told Phillip when he saw Him that he was seeing the Father (John 14:9). Should it not follow that when an unbeliever sees a Christian, he would think of Jesus? This provokes me to ask myself: Do others see Jesus in me; do I "re-present" Him in my words and in my works; am I bringing glory to the Father?

Jesus promised that the Holy Spirit would be my Helper, my guide, and my leader and that He would empower me to become all He has ordained for me before the foundation of the world (John 14:16–17; Acts 1:8; Eph. 2:10). Am I "co-operating" with the Holy Spirit; am I on "co-mission" with Him? If not, why not? Have I set up some "high places" that are taking the place of my God? Am I really a "sweet tater" or just a "spec-tater" with my eyes focused on *me*?

It should be no surprise that "sin" is spelled s-I-n ("I" in the middle). If we replace the "I" with an "O," we get s-O-n, the "Son," the One who releases us from the sin that separates us from God. We hear the argument so often that there are many ways to God, but the Word says that there is only one way and His name is Jesus. He proclaims in John 14:6:

> I am the way, the truth, and the life. No one comes to the Father except through Me.

It's not bragging when it's the truth!

In Hebrews 9:22 we are told that without the shedding of blood there is no remission of sin, and following verses (23–28) speak of the greatness of Christ's sacrifice on the Cross of Calvary.

> For Christ has not entered the holy places made with hands, which are copies of the true, but into heaven itself, now to appear in the presence of God for us; not that He should offer Himself often, as the high priest enters the Most Holy Place every year with the blood of another—He then would have had to suffer often since the foundation of the world, but now, once at the end of the ages, He has appeared to put away sin by the sacrifice of Himself. And as it is appointed for men to die once, but after this the judgment, so Christ was offered once to bear the sins of many. To those who eagerly wait for Him He will appear a *second time*, apart from sin, for salvation.
> —HEBREWS 9:24–28, EMPHASIS ADDED

Recently I was burdened in my heart for those in prison because of their faith, and then those in prison because of their transgression of the laws of the land. As I was meditating, the Lord spoke to my spirit these words:

> There are two kingdoms on earth, the Kingdom of Light and the Kingdom of Darkness. Many are in prisons not made of bars, but prisons of fear, unforgiveness and sin; they have chosen to dwell in the Kingdom of Darkness. Many are in prisons of bars, but they are free, because they know the Truth, and the Truth sets them free; they have chosen the Kingdom of Light. I AM the Way, the Truth, the Life—and the Light!

Let's look at the back of the Book and get a preview of this "second time" we just read about in Hebrews, confirming that Jesus Christ is the way:

> Now I saw heaven opened, and behold, a white horse. And He who sat on him was called Faithful and True…and His name is called The Word of God.
> —REVELATION 19:11, 13

Only the Father knows when the Second Coming of Christ will be. Our instructions in Luke 19:13 (KJV) are to "occupy" (like soldiers occupy the land they have conquered). Joshua, successor of Moses and a mighty warrior of God, was told four times in the first chapter of Joshua to be strong and courageous (vv. 6, 7, 9, 18); and the way he would be able to accomplish this was by meditating on the Word day and night and observing and doing all that was written in it (v. 8).

Paul tells us that "all Scripture is given by inspiration of God, and is profitable for doctrine, for reproof, for correction, for instruction in righteousness" (2 Tim. 3:16).

The scriptures are for our edification and are "profitable," building us up in Christ.

A main piece of the armor of God is described in Ephesians 6:17 as the "sword of the Spirit, which is the word of God." Christians are armed and dangerous!

As Christians we are in the world but not of the world (see Romans 12:2); therefore, we get dusty and dirty. We are cleansed "with the washing of water by the word" (Eph. 5:26).

It can be a bit overwhelming if we look at our Christian walk long range. The hardest part of our life here on earth is that it is so daily—24/7. But that is how we must take it—day by day. This is an old saying and so true: "Life by the inch is a cinch, but life by the yard is hard." I once was lamenting what was in my future when the Lord said: "Don't worry so much about the future. I know the future and you know Me!" We are to rest in Him and let Him work through us by the power of the Holy Spirit. He just wants "F-A-T" Christians: faithful, available, and teachable. Jesus said that we are to take no thought about tomorrow (Matt. 6:34). We are not to worry about it because worry never changes anything. It's like rocking in a rocking chair—keeps you busy but you don't get anywhere.

I have been taught that if you want to know the heart and mind of God, read five psalms and one chapter of Proverbs each day; you will complete the books in thirty days. It works really well until you get to Psalm 119. Because it is lengthy, you are tempted to hurry through, but it is well worth the time and effort. Word in = Word out. When we get bumped, we will not spill out the bitter words of the world but the sweet words of God's Holy Bible, precious words of life.

To trust in someone's word, we must believe his word

to be trustworthy. In many episodes of *Little House on the Prairie*, a television show about the early days of the West, you would hear Charles Ingalls, who played the father, say, "You have my word." His word carried weight because he was a man of integrity.

As children, when we wanted to put emphasis on our promises, we would say: "Cross my heart and hope to die; stick a needle in my eye." We were giving our word, and it was more important than life or pain (according to our limited knowledge). We have the Cross of Christ and we can safely stand on the integrity of His Word. After all, He is the Word (John 1:1).

I was having a discussion with a friend, and we were at odds about whether a certain thing was right or wrong. I kept quoting the Bible as my source, and the other person recanted, "But we must be tolerant." I did not want to argue and let the matter drop. I later sought the Lord's counsel and heard in my spirit: "Keep My Word and My Word will keep you."

I was on safe ground in quoting the Word, because that is precisely what Jesus did in a confrontation with Satan (Luke 4:1–13). After His baptism by John the Baptist and being filled with the Holy Spirit, He was led by the Holy Spirit into the wilderness where He was tempted by Satan for forty days, during which time He ate nothing.

At the end of those days, he was hungry and then Satan came, tempting Jesus to turn the stones into bread. Jesus declined, saying, "It is written" (Luke 4:4). Satan then offered to Jesus power over all the kingdoms of the world if He would worship him. Jesus rebuked him, saying "It is written" (v. 8). And then Satan dared Jesus to throw Himself from the pinnacle of the temple to prove He is the Son of God, and Satan himself says, "It is written" (v. 10), quoting a portion from Psalm 91:11–12 about angels' protection; however, he does not quote verbatim.

Satan used the same approach with Eve in the garden: "Has God indeed said?" (Gen. 3:1). Could Satan possibly think that Jesus, the Word, does not know the Word? Jesus at last answers: "It has been said, 'You shall not tempt the Lord your God'" (v. 12), and Satan departs "until an opportune time" (v. 13).

It does not take a rocket scientist to teach us the importance of the Word of God as the source of all we need to walk in victory until our Lord comes for us, in all His glory. James 1:2–4 tells us:

> My brethren, count it all joy when you fall into various trials, knowing that the testing of your faith produces patience. But let patience have its perfect work, that you may be perfect and complete, lacking nothing.

Our Lord is bringing us to maturity—building our character, and many times it is a painful process. The end result, however, is a harvest of "sweet taters."

## Parable of Sweet Iced Tea

A favorite drink here in the South is sweet iced tea. There is a secret to really good sweet iced tea: you must put the sugar in and stir while the tea is hot. That way the sugar will dissolve and permeate the tea; they become one. If you wait and put the sugar in when the tea is cold, all the sugar will settle at the bottom; it will not dissolve and become a part of the tea; there are two parts.

Is this not a parable for our lives? When we are in the refiner's fire, His Spirit pours into us, stirs us, and as we submit, He transforms us and we become one with Him. If we remain cold and refuse to submit to the fire, resisting the Spirit's call, we will remain divided—tea on top, sugar at the bottom—bitter to the taste.

Chapter 11

# ANOTHER THING ABOUT TATERS

**T**ATERS ARE NOT to be eaten raw. They can be prepared in many ways, including baked, boiled, and fried. Depending on your recipe, you leave the skin on or off. A baked potato needs to be scrubbed before it is put into a very hot oven, about 400 degrees. You can wrap it in foil and punch holes in it with a fork to let the steam out while it is baking. To test whether it is fully baked, you squeeze it with your fingers to make sure it is soft and fully cooked. You serve it with salt, pepper and butter and perhaps add toppings of your choice, such as sour cream, bacon, chives, cheese, chili, or broccoli. You can dress it any way you like.

Mashed potatoes must be washed, peeled, cut into cubes, and boiled until done before they are mashed with either a potato masher or whipped with a beater. Add salt, pepper, butter, and milk. They are not supposed to be "lumpy." (I served mashed potatoes to a young youth pastor who ate with us one Sunday after church. He said he loved the potatoes because of the little lumps. I took this as a compliment.) Another neat thing about mashed potatoes is that you can take the leftovers, mix with egg and flour, make patties, and fry them in hot oil, giving you potato pancakes or potato patties—your call.

Scalloped potatoes require you to peel the potatoes and pare them into thin slices. Layer the pieces in a greased baking pan, topping each layer of potatoes with flour, milk, salt, and pepper. You can add cheese shortly before the potatoes are done if desired.

French fries usually are peeled potatoes cut into strips, but if you wish, you can leave the skin on. They are put into hot oil and fried until crispy and golden. Then add salt, and if you wish, you can dip them in ketchup.

Hash browns are shredded potatoes that are clumped into patties and fried in hot oil. Add salt and pepper.

Small boiled potatoes, once they are cooled, can be cut into small pieces to make potato salad. You can add pickles, onions, celery, and boiled eggs, as you choose, to complete the salad.

Boiled potatoes can also be added to green beans and served together, or you can just top them with butter, add salt and pepper, and serve them as a side vegetable.

Thus you have the tater. But, as you can see, in order to be tasty, it requires some work. Depending on its assignment, it must be scrubbed, perhaps peeled, baked, boiled, or fried. Like the sweet iced tea, heat is required. The tater does not stand alone, but various condiments and other ingredients are added.

Perhaps you have heard it said, "God loves you just the way you are; but He loves you too much to leave you that way." We come into His kingdom as baby Christians, but we have assignments (recipes). Each person is born "for such a time as this," like Queen Esther (Esther 4:14). God determines our "preappointed times and the boundaries of [our] dwellings" (Acts 17:26). He also chooses the "good works, which God prepared beforehand that we should walk in them" (Eph. 2:10).

In order to fulfill our destiny and complete our "recipes," we must be processed; we cannot remain raw or half-baked. Some things must be deleted, such as dirt and hard skins;

and other things must be added, such as "love, joy, peace, longsuffering, kindness, goodness, faithfulness, gentleness, self-control" (Gal. 5:22–23). The fire will burn off the dross (Isa. 1:25) and make us pure and fit for the work of the kingdom.

An admirer was asking the sculptor of a magnificent horse how he created such a masterpiece. The artist replied: "I simply cut away everything that wasn't horse." Is that not what our Lord does in our lives—the Holy Spirit simply cuts away everything in us that is not like Jesus or that Jesus would not like.

> For whom He foreknew, He also predestined to be conformed to the image of His Son, that He might be the firstborn among many brethren.
>
> —ROMANS 8:29

# Am I Done Yet?

"Am I done yet?" the Tater asks the Master Chef;
"Not quite," He replies as He takes tongs from the
shelf.
"But Lord, I've been in here so long, and the fire is
hot!"
"Be patient, Little One; you must be prepared for the
pot.
"A heap of love, mounds of joy and peace, a smidgen
of salt,
A tablespoon of kindness, shovels of self-control over
your thoughts—
It will all come together in the fullness of My time;
And you will be pleased with this dish so sublime—
For it will spur the appetites of those far and near
To come to the Table of Grace, where there is no
sorrow or tear,
To feast with the Father, the Spirit and the Son,
As you hear the words, "Faithful Servant, well done!"

# Chapter 12
## GOD'S PEAS

J UST LIKE "TATERS," peas require some preparation before they are ready to be served. They must be washed, steamed and/or boiled, and seasoned. Of course, you need a clean container. Paul writes to Timothy about being "a vessel for honor, sanctified and useful for the Master, prepared for every good work" (2 Tim. 2:21).

The list of peas is endless, but here are a few: black-eyed, butter, crowder, English, field, and lady. In the South we have "goober peas," which are really peanuts.

To have some fun, we could compare the black-eyed pea to the "Spec-Tater." We are called to get involved, not just be spectators. It is a tradition on New Year's Day to eat black-eyed peas because for every pea you eat, in the coming year you will get a dollar.

Butter peas are just yummy and high class. Mother Hattie would serve them with Thanksgiving dinner. Doesn't our Lord call us to "come up here" (Rev. 4:1); we are "King's Kids."

Crowder peas could represent the crowds that followed Jesus, to see His miracles and hear Him teach. There was a huge crowd on the day He fed the five thousand (not counting the women and children) with just five loaves and two fishes, and crowds followed Jesus to see Him perform miracles.

English peas—how formal! This makes me think of Galatians 3:28:

> There is neither Jew nor Greek, there is neither slave nor free, there is neither male nor female; for you are all one in Christ Jesus.

So a pea by any other name is still a pea.

Field peas are a reminder of the harvest fields. Jesus admonished us to "pray the Lord of the harvest to send out laborers into His harvest" (Matt. 9:38). Jesus also said:

> Again, the kingdom of heaven is like treasure hidden in a field, which a man found and hid; and for joy over it he goes and sells all that he has and buys that field.
> —MATTHEW 13:44

Lady peas could well apply to the Proverbs 31 woman that we hear as the topic of sermons on Mother's Day. This gal can be mighty hard to measure up to, since she is trustworthy and industrious; she is a smart shopper and a good cook; she manages her household well, invests in real estate, gardens, works out, stays up late to do her work, sews, does volunteer charity work, and supports her husband in his career; she never says a bad word about anybody, minds her own business; she is never lazy, has perfect children and a perfect marriage. This is why many women do not like to come to church on Mother's Day! A friend of mine testifies that for a long time she hated this Proverbs 31 wonder woman, but one day the Lord changed her heart and she saw the lady in a different perspective. Not every woman can meet all the criteria in verses 10–29; however, verses 30 and 31 set us free:

Charm is deceitful and beauty is vain, But a woman who fears the Lord, *she* shall be praised. Give her the fruit of *her hands*, And let *her own* works praise her in the gates.
—Proverbs 31:30–31, emphasis added

It's our own personal relationship with the Lord that counts—how we reverence and honor Him. We each have gifts that are unique to us, given to us by the Holy Spirit at His discretion; therefore, it is a waste of time to compare ourselves with others.

But one and the same Spirit works all these things, distributing to each one individually as He wills.
—1 Corinthians 12:11

It is quite all right if you do not like to sew or garden or invest in real estate and all that other good stuff, including exercise (even though it is good for you). I personally think the earth would tilt to one side if we were all the same, plus it would be very boring.

My gardener friend says that for a plant to thrive, it must be in a "happy place." Paul found his "happy place" for he said:

Not that I speak in regard to need, for I have learned in whatever state I am, to be content.
—Philippians 4:11

Our Lord likes variety in His garden. An old saying is to just "bloom where you are planted," and that is very good advice. If you're a daisy, be the best daisy you can be and don't waste time lamenting that you are not a rose. God looks at us with eyes of love; we are each one of a kind.

Southerners know that "goober peas" are not really peas at all—they are peanuts. The term comes from the days of the Civil War. The Confederate soldiers, "after being cut off from the rail lines and their farm land, they had little to eat aside from boiled peanuts (or "goober peas"), which often served as an emergency ration."[1]

Goober peas can also be parched, which means you place the raw peanuts in a single layer on a cookie sheet in an oven heated to 350 degrees for about twenty minutes. Resist the heavenly smell and let them cool before you eat.

These are some of the peas in our food chain; and they, like the taters, need some refiner's fire to bring out their best. However, our Lord has some "P's" that He graciously provides as good gifts to His children. His "P's" do not need to be embellished; we simply take and appropriate them as our own.

> Every good and perfect gift is from above, and comes down from the Father of lights, with whom there is no variation or shadow of turning.
> —JAMES 1:17

# ADD PEAS TO THOSE TATERS

Man shall not live by taters alone,
Add some peas and corn pone.
Have a bowl of parched goober peas,
And wash it all down with sweet iced tea.

That will keep you going for awhile,
But for a life that is really worthwhile,
You need God's "P's":
Promises, Prayer, Protection, Provision,
Perseverance, Power in Praise, Promotion,
And Party Time!

P.S.: My friend Harry says that you cannot serve peas without taters because the taters hold the peas on the fork; otherwise, they'd be in your lap!

# Chapter 13

## PROMISES

THOUGHT I WOULD begin this section with the definition of *promise*; and I had to laugh when the definition
in *The American Century Dictionary* which followed
the word *promise* was "Promised Land."[1]

You must admit that the particular promise of God to
give certain land to Abraham and his seed (Israelites) is
still a major bone of contention between not just Israel
and the Palestinians but the whole world. This Promised
Land was not some vacant property waiting for tenants;
it was already occupied by some other "ites"—Canaanites,
Hittites, Amorites, Perizzites, Hivites, and Jebusites (Judg.
3:5). And these "ites" were reluctant, to say the least, to
hand over their land to these upstart Israelites. The Book
of Joshua chronicles these battles, but there is a current
ongoing battle.

We hear in the news that peace talks are underway with
the view of a possible peace treaty in 2014; however, the one
big obstacle is Jerusalem, because both sides want her and
Israel refuses to divide the city, their capitol.

The Lord spoke specifically about Jerusalem saying:

> Behold, I will make Jerusalem a cup of drunkenness
> to all the surrounding peoples, when they lay siege
> against Judah and Jerusalem. And it shall happen in
> that day that I will make Jerusalem a heavy stone for
> all peoples; all who would heave it away will surely be

cut in pieces, though all nations of the earth are gathered against it…In that day the LORD will defend the inhabitants of Jerusalem; the one who is feeble among them in that day shall be like David, and the house of David shall be like God, like the Angel of the LORD before them. In shall be in that day that I will seek to destroy all the nations that come against Jerusalem.

—ZECHARIAH 12: 2–3, 8–9

But let's get back to the definitions, just to keep things orderly. The definition of promise: "assurance that one will or will not undertake a certain action, etc.; potential for achievement; to make a promise; seem likely (to); *assure*"[2] (emphasis added). The definition of *Promised Land*: "Canaan, land *promised by* God to Abraham and his people; *fervent goal*"[3] (emphasis added).

God's covenant people can be *assured* that they will inherit the *promise*; they will achieve their *fervent* goal because God said so!

God is not a man, that He should lie, Nor the son of man, that he should repent. Has He said, and will He not do? Or has He spoken, and will He not make it good?

—NUMBERS 23:19

Is He able to keep His promise? Just ask Job. During his time of testing, Job yearned to speak to God, to get some answers to his dilemma. At last he did!

Then the LORD answered Job out of the whirlwind, and said: "Who is this who darkens counsel By words without knowledge? Now prepare yourself like a man; I will question you, and you shall answer Me."

—JOB. 38:1–3

The Lord asks Job some basic questions about creation, for instance:

> Where were you when I laid the foundations of the earth? Tell Me, if you have understanding. Who determined its measurements? Surely you know!
>
> —JOB 38:4–5

The Lord proceeds to discuss the earth's measurements, foundations, and cornerstone; the sea and the boundaries of its proud waves; the morning and the dawn, light and darkness and snow, the winds and the rain and the planets, among other things. And then the Lord takes Job to the zoo and shows him the various animals and birds. (See Job 38:6–41; 39:1–30.) The Lord concludes:

> Shall the one who contends with the Almighty correct Him? He who rebukes God, let him answer it.
>
> —JOB 40:2

The Lord challenges Job and concludes by taking Job to Jurassic Park, describing behemoth and leviathan (Job 40:8–14; 41:1–34). Job then answered the Lord:

> I know that You can do everything, And that no purpose of Yours can be withheld from You.
>
> —JOB 42:1–2

You can ask me also, for I most assuredly testify that not one of God's promises to me has ever failed. Do I get an "Amen"?

God Himself initiated this Abrahamic Covenant. In Genesis 17:4–8 we read:

> As for Me, behold, My covenant is with you, and you shall be a father of many nations. No longer will

your name be called Abram, but your name shall be Abraham; for I have made you a father of many nations. I will make you exceedingly fruitful; and I will make nations of you, and kings shall come from you. And I will establish My covenant between Me and you and your descendants after you in their generations, for an everlasting covenant, to be God to you and your descendants after you. Also I give to you and your descendants after you the land in which you are a stranger, all the land of Canaan, as an everlasting possession; and I will be their God.

The Lord cautioned Abraham that it would take some time before the promise would be fulfilled.

Know certainly that your descendants will be strangers in a land that is not theirs [Egypt], and will serve them, and they will afflict them four hundred years. And also the nation whom they serve I will judge; afterward they shall come out with great possessions.

—Genesis 15:13–14

In Exodus 12:40–41 we are told:

Now the sojourn of the children of Israel who dwelt in Egypt was four hundred and thirty years [altogether, that is, from the time of the covenant until they left Egypt]. And it came to pass at the end of the four hundred and thirty years—on that very same day—it came to pass that all the armies of the LORD went out from the land of Egypt.

At one point Moses sent twelve spies into the land of Canaan, but ten returned with a bad report. Only Joshua and Caleb urged the Israelites to take the land the Lord had given them. The majority refused to enter Canaan; and because of their rebellion, the Lord banished them to wander in the wilderness for forty years, one year for each day in which they spied out the land. Only Joshua, Caleb, and those who were children at that time would inherit the Promised Land (Num. 14:26–38).

> After the death of Moses, the servant of the LORD, it came to pass that the LORD spoke to Joshua the son of Nun, Moses' assistant, saying: "Moses, my servant is dead. Now therefore, arise, go over this Jordan, you and all this people, to the land which I am giving to them—the children of Israel. Every place that the sole of your foot will tread upon I have given you, as I said to Moses. From the wilderness of this Lebanon as far as the great river, the River Euphrates, all the land of the Hittites and to the Great Sea toward the going down of the sun, shall be your territory. No man shall be able to stand before you all the days of your life; as I was with Moses, so I will be with you. I will not leave you nor forsake you. *Be strong and of good courage*, for to this people you shall divide as an inheritance the land which I swore to their fathers to give them.
> —JOSHUA 1:1–6, EMPHASIS ADDED

It is most interesting to note that three times in the first nine verses of Joshua 1, the Lord tells Joshua: "Be strong and of good courage" (vv. 6, 7, 9). He is moving closer to the fulfillment of the promise, but there is still much to be done and Joshua is not to faint or lose heart.

After many battles covering approximately thirty years, the covenant promise was fulfilled:

So the LORD gave to Israel all the land of which He had sworn to give to their fathers, and they took possession of it, and dwelt in it. The LORD gave them rest all around, according to all that He had sworn to their fathers. And not a man of all their enemies stood against them; the LORD delivered all their enemies into their hand. Not a word failed of any good thing which the LORD had spoken to the house of Israel. All came to pass.

—JOSHUA 21:43–45

Unfortunately, the Israelites were unable to keep their inheritance, and they were dispersed into foreign lands. Still, there was God's promise of restoration:

For I will take you from among the nations, gather you out of all countries, and bring you into your own land...Then you shall dwell in the land that I gave to your fathers; you shall be my people and I will be your God.

—EZEKIEL 36:24, 28

This prophecy was fulfilled on May 14, 1948, at 4:32 p.m., with the rebirth of the State of Israel.[4] Isaiah 66:8 records: "Can a county be born in a day?" (NIV).

John Hagee writes: "Jerusalem was reunited under Jewish leadership for the first time in two thousand years with Israel's victory in the Six-Day War of 1967. The Bible says, 'And Jerusalem will be trampled by Gentiles, until the time of the Gentiles are fulfilled' (Luke 21:24). If you listen closely you can hear the footsteps of Messiah walking toward Israel."[5]

I was privileged to be at the Wailing Wall in Jerusalem in April 1995, when our group was asked to move to the side because a delegation had arrived, escorting recent immigrants from Ethiopia. They were a sight to see—tall, black men dressed in flowing white robes and smiling from ear to ear. The Jewish escorts were excited, and it was contagious. Their brothers had come home, just as the Lord had promised.

I dearly love to get promises fulfilled quickly, but I find that most promises require some time and seasoning. The one for which I waited the longest (thirty years) was the restoration of my marriage. Bob had divorced me after twenty-eight years of marriage, but I had the Lord's promise that He would walk with me to the other side and one day I would have a good marriage. And one day, I did! But it was not as I had envisioned. I was with Bob at the end of his life, and I got my miracle when he asked that I forgive him for all the hurt and pain and said he had never stopped loving me. We had ten precious days reliving our good old days, and we agreed that we were soul mates. I was by his side when the Lord took him home. Now he is waiting for me, and I think that's fair. After all, I waited for him thirty years so now he can wait for me. Jesus and Bob are building my mansion in glory; after all, Jesus is a Master Carpenter.

It is clear to see that God's delay is not His denial. He is simply working all things "together for good to those who love God, to those who are the called according to His purpose" (Rom. 8:28). Our Lord does not waste anything. As He works, He conforms us to the image of Jesus (His divine nature), trimming away those things that are not like Him. When we are "done," the promise is fulfilled—right on time. Our Lord is patient to assure that His taters are not half-baked.

Simon Peter, an apostle of Jesus Christ, writes to the believers:

Grace and peace be multiplied to you in the knowledge of God and of Jesus our Lord, as His divine
power *has given to us all things that pertain to life
and godliness,* through the knowledge of Him who
called us by glory and virtue, by which *have been
given to us exceedingly great and precious promises
that through these you may be partakers of the divine
nature,* having escaped the corruption that is in the
world through lust.

—2 PETER 1:2–4, EMPHASIS ADDED

Do you see that we already have at our disposal "all
things that pertain to life and godliness?" It's like having
a gift under the Christmas tree, wrapped with your name
on it. It is a beautiful package, but it is of no use until you
open it and receive it as your own. It's like having a check
from your rich uncle, made payable to you and signed by
him, but you never cash it. We can trust in the character of
our God, who owns all the silver and gold (Hag. 2:8); His
check is valid.

We have been given these "exceedingly great and precious promises," not just because our loving Father delights
to give gifts to His children (indeed, He does), but there is a
greater purpose. He wants us to be "partakers of the divine
nature." When we receive and apply these promises to our
lives, they are tools that mold our character. The world can
then look at our changed lives; and as we let our little lights
shine, they are drawn to the Light of the world, extending
His kingdom here on earth. We are blessed to be a blessing,
an instrument of God's grace.

The most precious promise ever in all of the universe
came when Christ died for us on the cross. When we
accept His death, burial, and resurrection in atonement
for our sins, we become "JRS." (This is speaking in today's

"tweeting," where you communicate in letters, not words.) JRS means we are JUSTIFIED (just-as-if-I-never-sinned); we are RECONCILED to God; and we are SAVED from wrath through Him.

Paul writes about this in Romans 5:

> For when we were still without strength, in due time Christ died for the ungodly. For scarcely for a righteous man will one die; yet perhaps for a good man someone would even dare to die. But God demonstrates His own love toward us, in that while we were still sinners Christ died for us. Much more then, having now been *justified* by His blood, we shall be *saved* from wrath through Him. For if when we were enemies we were *reconciled* to God through the death of His Son, much more, having been *reconciled*, we shall be saved by His life. And not only that, but we also rejoice in God through our Lord Jesus Christ, through whom we have now received the *reconciliation*.
>
> —ROMANS 5:6–11, EMPHASIS ADDED

This is the foundation we stand on as followers of Christ. Our sins have been removed and we have a relationship with Father God. We are JRS—justified, reconciled, and saved— because Jesus died in our place, and it was all because of love. When we "get it," then we share "it" with others. Love others into the kingdom with this good news; they can be JRS also. There's plenty of room at our Lord's table.

Jesus began to tell His disciples He would be departing soon; and they were dismayed, to say the least. Their leader was leaving, and without a head they would be dead. Then Jesus promised them another Helper, the Holy Spirit, who would abide with them forever and live in them

(John 4:16–17). This second Helper (Jesus was first) will continue to teach His disciples and bring to their remembrance all things that Jesus taught them (v. 26) so that they could in turn give us the inerrant Word of God (2 Pet. 1:20–21). He will convict the world of sin, of righteousness, and of judgment; He will guide us into all truth; He will show us things to come; He will glorify Christ; and He will take the things of Christ and show them to us (John 16:8–11, 13–15).

The Holy Spirit began His ministry on the Day of Pentecost, empowering the followers of Christ to be witnesses in Jerusalem, Judea, Samaria, and the uttermost parts of the world (Acts 1:8). Three thousand souls were added to the kingdom that day and the church was born (2:41).

Paul listed nine spiritual gifts of the Holy Spirit that equip us for ministry: word of wisdom, word of knowledge, faith, gifts of healing, working of miracles, prophecy, discerning of spirits, different kinds of tongues (languages), and interpretation of tongues (1 Cor. 12:8–10).

As we continue to abide in Him, we bear the fruit of the Spirit: "Love, joy, peace, longsuffering, kindness, goodness, faithfulness, gentleness, self-control" (Gal. 5:22–23). Paul calls love the "more excellent way" (1 Cor. 12:31).

Paul went on to say in Romans 5:3, 5:

> We also glory in tribulations…because the love of God has been poured out in our hearts by the Holy Spirit who was given to us.

This is a comforting promise in these days of trials and tribulations. The Helper fills our hearts with love, the most powerful force in the world. "God is love" (1 John 4:8)!

In the Book of Proverbs 4:7, we read:

Wisdom is the principal thing; therefore, get wisdom.
And in all your getting, get understanding.

How do you get wisdom? You just ask for it.

If any of you lacks wisdom, let him ask of God, who
gives to all liberally and without reproach, and it will
be given to him.

—James 1:5

King Solomon, the son of David and Bathsheba, was
wiser than all men, and also the richest. As he was about to
begin his reign as the king of Israel, the Lord appeared to
him in a dream by night; and God said, "Ask! What shall I
give you?"

And Solomon said: "You have shown great mercy to
your servant David my father, because he walked
before You in truth, in righteousness, and in upright-
ness of heart with You; You have continued this great
kindness to him, and You have given him a son to
sit on his throne, as it is this day. Now, O LORD my
God, You have made Your servant a king instead of
my father David, but I am a little child; I do not know
how to go out or come in. And Your servant is in the
midst of Your people whom You have chosen, a great
people, too numerous to be numbered or counted.
Therefore, give to Your servant an understanding
heart to judge Your people, that I may discern
between good and evil. For who is able to judge this
great people of Yours?" The speech pleased the Lord,
that Solomon had asked this thing. Then God said to
him: "Because you have asked this thing, and have
not asked long life for yourself, nor have asked riches
for yourself, nor have asked the life of your enemies,
but have asked for yourself understanding to discern

justice, behold, I have done according to your words;
see, I have given you a wise and understanding heart,
so that there has not been anyone like you before
you, nor shall any like you arise after you. And I have
also given you what you have not asked: both riches
and honor, so that there shall not be anyone like you
among the kings all your days."

—1 Kings 3:6–13

Continuing we find God's answer:

And God gave Solomon wisdom and exceedingly
great understanding and largeness of heart, like
the sand on the seashore. Thus Solomon's wisdom
excelled the wisdom of all the men of the East and
all the wisdom of Egypt. For he was wiser than all
men…He spoke three thousand proverbs, and his
songs were one thousand and five.

—1 Kings 4:29–32

Jesus taught this same principle about asking in
Matthew 7:7–8:

Ask, and it will be given unto you; seek and you
will find; knock, and it will be opened to you. For
everyone who asks receives, and he who seeks finds,
and to him who knocks it will be opened.

"A" is for ask; "S" is for seek; and "K" is for knock, which
equals ASK. Jesus went on to say (Matt. 7:11) that even an
evil father will give good gifts to his children; therefore,
"how much more will your Father who is in heaven give
good gifts to those who ask Him!"

Do you long for rest in these hectic days? Jesus extends
this invitation in Matthew 11:28–30:

Come to Me, all you who labor and are heavy laden, and I will give you rest. Take My yoke upon you and learn from Me, for I am gentle and lowly in heart, and you will find rest for your souls. For My yoke is easy and My burden is light.

There is a flip side to this promise of rest. We spoke earlier of the Promised Land and how God kept His Word through Joshua; however, not all who started completed the journey. As believers, we are promised eternal rest through our belief in the finished work of our Lord Jesus Christ.

It is said: "Today, if you will hear His voice, do not harden your hearts as in the rebellion." For who, having heard, rebelled? Indeed, was it not all who came out of Egypt, led by Moses. Now with whom was He angry forty years? Was it not with those who sinned, whose corpses fell in the wilderness? And to whom did He swear that they would not enter His rest, but to those who did not obey? So we see that they could not enter in because of unbelief... Therefore, since a promise remains of entering His rest, let us fear lest any of you seem to have come short of it. For indeed the gospel was preached to us as well as to them; but the word which they heard did not profit them, not being mixed with faith in those who hear it. For we who have believed do enter that rest... The works were finished from the foundation of the world... There remains therefore a rest for the people of God. For he who has entered His rest has himself also ceased from his works as God did from His. Let us therefore be diligent to enter that rest, lest anyone fall according to the same example of disobedience.

—HEBREWS 3:15–19; 4:1–3, 9–11

This promise of rest brings to my mind the 23rd Psalm, where we see Jesus as the Good Shepherd, tenderly caring for His flock. The last line reads:

> *Surely* [absolutely, positively] goodness and mercy shall follow me *all* the days of my life; and I will dwell [rest] in the house of the Lord *forever.*
>
> —PSALM 23:6, EMPHASIS ADDED

This would be a sweet, comforting way to end the "rest" promise, *but* (there are "holy Buts" in the Bible, you know) has the Lord ever applied verse 2 of Psalm 23 to your life? That's where "He *makes* me to lie down in green pastures" (emphasis added)? We don't want to lie down; we want to keep going full steam ahead, doing things our way instead of "Yah-weh."

I remember vividly, although this has been many years ago, when I had three small children and I was frazzled. I had asked the Lord for rest, but I should have been more specific. The family was playing in the stream that ran over the rocks at Indian Springs, when my brother-in-law tried to push my niece into the water. As she was trying to keep her balance, she grabbed me and I landed headfirst on the rocks. This required eighteen stitches in my head and resulted in some forced rest. I had been made to lie down; but the pastures were green, not barren, for I learned a valuable lesson: space myself, pray specifically, and get proper rest. After all, dust will keep if it doesn't get wet.

Our world today is crying for peace. The Middle East at the time of this writing is a boiling cauldron, which is just another sign of the times. And we say, what else is new? It will be this way until Jesus, the Prince of Peace, comes.

When the disciples were in the boat, going to the other

side of the lake, just as Jesus instructed, a great storm arose and they were frightened (Mark 4:35–40).

> He [Jesus] was in the stern, asleep on a pillow. And they awoke Him and said to Him, "Teacher, do you not care that we are perishing?" Then He arose and rebuked the wind, and said to the sea, "Peace, be still!" And the wind ceased and there was a great calm. But He said to them, "How is it that you have no faith?"
> —MARK 4:38–40

Jesus had said they were going to the other side, but they did not trust His word; they were looking at circumstances. And so do we!

Paul writes about Christ, our peace:

> For He Himself is our peace, who has made both one, and has broken down the middle wall of separation, having abolished in His flesh the enmity, that is, the law of commandments contained in ordinances, so as to create in Himself one new man from the two, thus making peace, and that He might reconcile them both to God in one body through the cross, thereby putting to death the enmity. And He came and preached peace to you who were afar off and to those who were near. For through Him we both have access by one Spirit to the Father.
> —EPHESIANS 2:14–18

We must stay focused on our Lord, not the winds, the waves and the water, because:

> You will keep him in perfect peace, Whose mind is stayed on You, Because he trusts in you.
> —ISAIAH 26:3

Our strength also comes from our Lord:

> Fear not, for I am with you; Be not dismayed, for I
> am the Lord your God. I will strengthen you, Yes, I
> will help you. I will uphold you with My righteous
> right hand [the hand of blessing].
> —ISAIAH 41:10

I read once that there are 365 "fear nots" in the Bible—
one for each day of the year.

He comforts us and then, not wasting anything, He uses
us to comfort others:

> Blessed be the God and Father of our Lord Jesus
> Christ, the Father of mercies and God of all comfort,
> who comforts us in all our tribulation, that we may
> be able to comfort those who are in any trouble, with
> the comfort with which we ourselves are comforted
> by God. For as the sufferings of Christ abound in us,
> so our consolation also abounds through Christ.
> —2 CORINTHIANS 1:3–5

Don't we get the greatest comfort from those who have
been there and done that?

We also have the promise of forgiveness:

> If we confess our sins, *He is faithful* and just to forgive
> us our sins and to cleanse us from all unrighteousness.
> —1 JOHN 1:9, EMPHASIS ADDED

The Bible itself is a book of promises given to us by the
Promise Keeper, who watches over His word and hastens
to perform it (Jer. 1:12), even if we are slow, because some
promises are conditional. We can safely stand on His promises because "He is faithful." No book could contain all the

"exceedingly great and precious promises" (2 Pet. 1:4) that our Lord has given to us in His Word and personally to His children, but here is a real "doozy" that you can hang your hat on:

> Trust in the L<small>ORD</small>, and do good; dwell in the land, and feed on His faithfulness. Delight yourself also in the Lord, And He shall give you the desires of your heart. Commit your way to the Lord, Trust also in Him, And He shall bring it to pass.
> —P<small>SALM</small> 37:3–5

Our part is to trust, put our faith in the One who is trustworthy. We are to "do good" because He is good, and we are "imi-taters" of the Lord; His goodness is in us and flows out of us, especially when we are bumped. We "dwell" or "abide" in Him and "feed" on His faithfulness, not our own; like sheep in the field of the Good Shepherd. To "delight" is to be enthusiastic or excited. For instance, a plain vanilla cone from the Dairy Queen is nice, but when it's dipped in chocolate—that's "delight-full!" We "commit" our ways to Him and like in the John Wayne movies, we totally surrender. When we do all these verbs: trust, do, dwell, feed, delight, and commit, then our hearts will match His heart, and He can safely give us those desires because He planted them there in the first place.

I know you can see from the preceding paragraph that I do love chocolate. I think it is one of the most delightful gifts our Lord has given us to enjoy. My favorite candy bar is Snickers. Sometimes for variety I will choose a Baby Ruth or a Butterfinger. But, if my Father owns the candy store, I can have the "desires of my heart." All the candy is at my disposal, within reason, of course. To eat too much would not be good for me. It is the presence of the Father and my relationship with Him that makes the difference.

Take special note of this last recorded promise of our Lord Jesus in Matthew 28:20: "And lo, *I am* with you always, even to the end of the age" (emphasis added). He is the "*I AM*," and that is open-ended. He is present tense; He is everything you need. *I AM* your banker; *I AM* your healer; *I AM* your provider; *I AM* your comforter; *I AM* your strength; *I AM* your guide; *I AM* your teacher; *I AM* (you name it). And He is "with us," not against us! *Always!*

## THE FIELD OF PROMISES

The Father planted a field of promises for His
    daughters and sons;
Every need is supplied in its own special section.
It is verdant with wisdom, strength, joy, and peace,
And baskets are provided, so take as much as you
    wish.

To access this field there is but one qualification:
You must enter through the Door of Justification.
To harvest here requires Reconciliation,
But no need to fret—Jesus paid for your salvation.

Not just to give you "pie in the sky,"
And a mansion in the "sweet by-and-by,"
But to give you life—right here and now—
Abundant, rich, and overflowing—that's His vow!

Grab your coat and hat, take Jesus by the hand,
Go into the field, gather as much as you can
To share with the world, His people everywhere,
Because the more you give, the more will be there!

Chapter 14

# PRAYER

**P**RAYER IS SIMPLE, but then again, it is not. Prayer is talking and listening to God, having a dialogue with Him; it's communicating with our heavenly Father. There can be no relationship without communication. Since we have two ears and one mouth, it stands to reason that we should listen more than we talk; however, that is not usually the case. We go to the Lord with our gimme list (give me this, give me that). We should be reporting for duty and asking for His wish list, what is on His heart. But in His grace and mercy, He bends His ear to hear us when we pray, and He longs to give us the desires of our hearts. That is the nature of our Abba Father.

In addition, and it's a magnificent addition, at the right side of the Father, the side of blessing, stands our Lord Jesus Christ giving His approval to our prayers. "He always lives to make intercession for them" (Heb. 7:25). The "them" is you and me, those "pray-ers."

And don't forget the Holy Spirit, our Helper, who helps us pray when we don't know what to pray (Rom. 8:26–27); *and* we have the angels of the Father, who minister to the heirs of salvation (Heb. 1:14). What an arsenal we have at our disposal; it is no wonder that Satan hates and fears the prayers of the saints.

We could compare prayer to the umbilical cord of a pregnant woman. The cord connects the baby to the placenta of the mother. Blood comes from the baby to the placenta, and waste products from the baby's blood, including carbon dioxide, are transferred into the mother and breathed out through her lungs. Oxygen and nutrients go from the mother to the baby, so the baby is getting blood that has been purified. The cord has a protective coating, and is coiled like a spring, giving the baby freedom to move. The umbilical cord is the lifeline between the baby and the mother.[1] That belly-button is not just something we joke about, whether it is an "outie" or an "innie." It points us to our God's most amazing creation—a human being.

Charlotte Sanders Cushman wrote:

> It seems as if when God conceived the world, that
>     was Poetry,
> He formed it and that was Sculpture:
> He colored it, and that was Painting:
> He peopled it with living beings, and that was the
>     grand, divine, eternal Drama.[2]

Isn't prayer our lifeline as well? We must stay connected to the Godhead: Father, Son, and Holy Spirit. If there is no blood, there is no life (Deut. 12:23), and "without the shedding of blood there is no remission" (Heb. 9:22)—no purifying of sins. The Holy Spirit is our Helper and our guide, bringing conviction when we stray. We have freedom to move, because Jesus makes us "free indeed" (John 8:36). The branch must abide in, or stay connected to, the vine in order to thrive and bear fruit. Jesus declares:

> If you abide in Me, and My words abide in you, you
> will ask what you desire, and it shall be done for you.
> —JOHN 15:7

Boiled down, prayer is the divine connection.

The Lord gave me a "visual aid" this morning, a lesson from nature about the importance of the abiding, staying connected. It's my very own parable, and I delight to share it with you, my dear reader.

## Parable of the Daisy

There was a daisy in my garden today, whose face
    was on the ground.
"Oh, no," I cried, with my spirit cast down.
"You were made to dance in the wind, with your
    head held high,
Smiling at the sun with glee, fulfilling your destiny."

Then I saw the reason for this tragedy:

Its stem was bent, its lifeline was gone—
Its time on earth was almost done.

There is a lesson here to learn—
A truth for me to discern.

If I am to dance in the wind, with my head held
    high,
I must stay connected to the Son, keep Him always
    nigh!
As I let His life flow through me,
I shall fulfill my destiny!

If you had a choice to be living on earth at any specific time in history, when would it be? I always thought it would be awesome to be one of the disciples who walked with Jesus, to be close enough to touch Him, to hear His teachings and witness His miracles. As I have matured in my faith, I find that this present time is the best time, because if I had been a disciple of Jesus, my closeness would be limited by space and time. Now, however, He has given me His Holy Spirit to live inside of me, and Jesus is as near as the air I breathe. He is just a prayer away.

The disciples saw Jesus perform incredible miracles: He turned water into wine; raised the dead; healed the sick, blind, and paralyzed; cast out demons; multiplied loaves and fishes; calmed the raging storm; walked on water; and greatest of all, He changed hearts, gave hope, and showed the way to the Father. But they saw something else, something that made a deep impression—they saw how Jesus prayed.

He would go off by Himself, spending hours at a time in prayer, communing with the Father. Then He would come forth to be about His Father's business, whether it was teaching, healing, performing miracles, or making major decisions, such as where and when He was to go next or who to choose as disciples. For example: Do I go to Samaria and reveal Myself as Messiah to a certain woman at the well? Do I go to Lazarus now, or wait a few days? Do I have supper with a hated tax collector named Zacchaeus?

The disciples had a lightbulb moment: prayer works! The important thing for them to learn was how to pray; the works would flow from that. And so they said, "Lord, teach us to pray" (Luke 11:1). And Jesus gave them the model for prayer, "The Lord's Prayer:"

> Our Father in heaven, Hallowed be Your name. Your kingdom come. Your will be done. On earth as it is in heaven. Give us this day our daily bread. And forgive us our debts, As we forgive our debtors. And do not lead us into temptation, But deliver us from the evil

> one. For Yours is the kingdom and the power and the
> glory forever. Amen.
>
> —Matthew 6:9–13

As we analyze this prayer, verse by verse, we see that Jesus has covered all things well. In the Old Testament, we see God as all powerful, almighty, and a God to be approached in holy awe and reverence through blood sacrifices and the intercession of the priests. But in the New Testament, Jesus shows us that we have relationship with a Father and He has a family: "Our Father in heaven." We know that we can love and trust Him and, therefore, confidently ask for His kingdom to come on earth because we know it will be good. This would cover also our need for healing for others and for ourselves, because we know there is no sickness in heaven.

We need "daily bread," and He has the resources to supply our needs, and the love that cannot deny the needs of His children. We need forgiveness and to extend that forgiveness to others in order to be free ourselves and to keep the lines of communication open. Jesus is our sterling example of forgiveness. We need our Father's guidance and deliverance from Satan, who is seeking to devour us (1 Pet. 5:8).

We can pray this prayer with faith that we already have our answer because we trust in our Father's character and ability: "For Yours *is* [that's right here and now, always present tense—*I Am*] the kingdom and the power and the glory *forever* [never a time when His kingdom, power and glory do not exist]. *Amen* [that means: so be it, because our Father says so]!" (Matt. 6:13, emphasis added).

There is a very sad account of the last time that Jesus asked His disciples to watch and pray. He actually made the request three times. It was in the Garden of Gethsemane, prior to His arrest and subsequent crucifixion. They slept instead.

> Then Jesus came with them to a place called Gethsemane, and said to the disciples, "Sit here while I go and pray over there." And He took with Him Peter and the two sons of Zebedee, and He began to be sorrowful and deeply distressed. Then He said to them, "My soul is exceedingly sorrowful, even to death. Stay here and watch with Me." Then Jesus came with them to a place called Gethsemane, and said to the disciples, "Sit here while I go and pray over there." And He took with Him Peter and the two sons of Zebedee, and He began to be sorrowful and deeply distressed. Then He said to them, "My soul is exceedingly sorrowful, even to death. Stay here and watch with Me." Then He came to the disciples and found them sleeping, and said to Peter, "What! Could you not watch with Me one hour? Watch and pray, lest you enter into temptation. The spirit indeed is willing, but the flesh is weak." Again, a second time, He went away and prayed, saying, "O My Father, if this cup cannot pass away from Me unless I drink it, Your will be done." And He came and found them asleep again, for their eyes were heavy. So He left them, went away again, and prayed the third time, saying the same words. Then He came to His disciples and said to them, "Are you still sleeping and resting? Behold, the hour is at hand, and the Son of Man is being betrayed into the hands of sinners. Rise, let us be going. See, My betrayer is at hand."
>
> —MATTHEW 26:36–46

Surely the disciples were heartbroken because they had slept on the job, not realizing the gravity of the situation.

They had failed their Lord, but it was only temporary. Of the eleven disciples remaining, ten died as martyrs for their faith. Only John lived to an old age; but he suffered also for Christ, even being exiled on the Isle of Patmos, where he was given "The Revelation of Jesus Christ" (Rev. 1:1). Our God redeems!

I ask myself: How many times have I fallen asleep while praying, or failed to watch and intercede for others? How many days have I skipped in praying over my "lost list" and especially for my church, my pastor, the staff, teachers, and musicians? And what about God's word to pray first for those in authority over me (1 Tim. 2:1–2), such as my president, his family, his cabinet and staff, and the federal and state legislators? Am I praying for the "peace of Jerusalem" (Ps. 122:6)? And am I praying The Lord's Prayer daily? What makes me any different from those disciples that evening in the Garden of Gethsemane? After all, I have His Word written down and I am living post-resurrection. As I finish this paragraph, I repent, ask for forgiveness, and promise, with the Holy Spirit's help, to do better in this ministry of prayer. Praise the Lord for His amazing grace!

I do confess that I pray diligently every day for "me and mine." It is imperative that my family be covered, have that hedge around them. Satan challenged God, claiming that Job, whom God considered as His servant, "a blameless and upright man, one who fears God and shuns evil" (Job 1:8), was only serving because God had "made a hedge around him, around his household, and all around that he has on every side...blessed the work of his hands, and his possessions have increased in the land" (v. 10).

This Book of Job shows that through suffering there comes a deeper faith in God. It's when your *knower knows* and you cannot be shaken. Job concluded that he had "heard," but "now my eye sees You" (Job 42:5). However, the point here is that at the start of it all, in Job 1:10, there was the hedge, and it was there because of Job's relationship with God through his sacrifices and prayers for his family. A further illustration of the importance of prayer is found in Ephesians 6:10–20, where Paul is instructing the believers:

> Put on the whole armor of God, that you may be able to stand against the wiles of the devil. For we do not wrestle against flesh and blood, but against principalities, against powers of this age, against spiritual hosts of wickedness in the heavenly places. Therefore, take up the whole armor of God, that you may be able to withstand in the evil day, and having done all, to stand.
> —EPHESIANS 6:11–13

Note that Paul says the "whole armor," which would include both defensive and offensive; some pieces are for protection, while others are for conquest. In the account of David's victory over the giant Goliath (1 Sam. 17), we see that David came against the enemy in the Name of the Lord. He used his sling and a single stone to knock Goliath face down, and then he used Goliath's own sword to cut off his head. David was fully equipped for battle.

In Ephesians 6:14–17, Paul proceeds to describe the girdle (belt) of truth around the waist, the breastplate of righteousness, the gospel of peace for the feet, the shield of faith, the helmet of salvation, and the sword of the Spirit (Word of God). Paul would doubtless be using as an example the armor worn by the Roman soldiers who were occupying Israel at that time.

The belt of truth would be used to hold the armor tight

around the loins and to hold other small pieces of weaponry, such as daggers and knives, and for David, a sling. Jesus said, "I am the way, the truth, and the life" (John 14:6). This is the truth, like a belt, that clinches our victory.

The breastplate of righteousness came in two parts, front and back, to cover the major organs of the body, and it extended down to the legs. When we are in Christ Jesus, we are in right standing, or righteous, with God (1 Cor. 1:30).

Feet would be shod with boots that would come up the front part of the leg. The soles would protect the feet from thorns and rocks and would also provide traction so you would not slip and fall. The gospel, or good news, is that Jesus is our peace, who has broken down the wall of separation (Eph. 2:14); He is the Prince of Peace and His Kingdom shall last forever (Isa. 9:6–7).

The shield of faith was notched, so fellow soldiers would lock together to form a wall, knocking down all the fiery darts of the enemy. We are not in this battle alone. Our faith in Christ saves us (Eph. 2:8–9); and victories are won through faith.

The helmet of salvation would protect the mind, where battles are won or lost. As Christians, we are promised "the mind of Christ" (1 Cor. 2:16).

The sword of the Spirit is both defensive and offensive. It is the Word of God. "In the beginning was the Word, and the Word was with God, and the Word was God...And the Word became flesh and dwelt among us" (John 1:1, 14). We are talking about Jesus here! Through the inspiration of the Holy Spirit, the Word has been recorded for us and it shall never pass away (see Matthew 24:35, NIV).

After we are dressed for battle with the whole armor, we are told to pray. Note how in Ephesians 6 verse 18 immediately follows verse 17 as part of that sentence:

…praying always with all prayer and supplication in the Spirit, being watchful to the end with all perseverance and supplication for all the saints.

Prayer completes the whole armor; prayer not only for ourselves, but for our brothers and sisters. And here is Jesus again, for He said that we could ask in His name and we would receive (John 14:13-14).

The whole armor of God basically comes down to this one person: *Jesus!* All that we need on this earth to walk in victory has been provided by His incarnation, death, burial, and resurrection. David had it right when he ran toward Goliath, proclaiming victory through his covenant relationship with God, which was subsequently ratified by the blood of our Lord Jesus Christ.

Dr. Charles Stanley wrote the following article entitled "Praying On the Armor of God" (Eph. 6:13–18):

Prepare yourself for each day's spiritual challenges by making the following prayer part of your morning routine:

"Dear Lord, as I get out of bed today, I know I'm stepping onto a battlefield. But I also know You've given me everything I need to stand firm. So in the power of Your Holy Spirit, I put on the armor of God:

"First, I place the helmet of salvation on my head. Protect my mind and imagination. Guard my eyes, allowing no sin to creep in. Focus my thoughts on the things of God. Let the breastplate of righteousness keep my heart and emotions safe. I pray that I won't be governed by my feelings, but by truth. Wrap Your Word around me like a belt. And safeguard me from error. I put on the sandals of peace to guide my steps. Plant my feet in Your truth. Empower me to stand firm against attack.

"Next, I take up the shield of faith. Protect me from Satan's fiery arrows. Place me shoulder to shoulder with Your army to oppose the Devil's schemes. Finally, I take up the sword of the Spirit, Your Word. Help me to read the Bible in a fresh, exciting way so I will always be ready to deflect attacks and pierce hearts with Your truth.

"I know I'll face assaults today, Lord. But You've empowered me to stand firm. Give me strength for the battle today."

Without God's armor, you're as vulnerable as a soldier who goes into battle wearing only a bathing suit. Get dressed for success![3]

Are many Christians today like the emperor in the Hans Christian Andersen fairy tale *The Emperor's New Clothes*, who paraded through the streets of the city in his new suit of clothes, not realizing that he was naked? That is, until an innocent little boy cried out, "He doesn't have on any clothes at all!"

I often wondered about the line in the Lord's Prayer where we pray, "Lord, lead us not into temptation but deliver us from the evil one" (Matt. 6:13). Jesus on the cross has delivered us, but Satan is a trespasser. He doesn't play fair; he hits our weak spots. My chief weakness is that I am a perfectionist (obsessive, compulsive); therefore, I constantly second-guess myself. Did I say it right? Should I have said more, or less, or anything at all? A professor of mine once laughed that an O.C.D. student of hers would comb the fringe on the rug, and I asked myself, "What's wrong with that?" Accordingly, it is imperative that I never remove the helmet of salvation.

There is a very interesting account of Daniel having a great vision, which left him disturbed because he could not understand its meaning. He had prayed for wisdom, and at last an angel appeared to him, perhaps Gabriel. Continuing in Daniel 10:12–14:

> Then he said to me, "Do not fear, Daniel, for from the first day that you set your heart to understand, and to humble yourself before your God, your words were heard; and I have come because of your words. But the prince of the kingdom of Persia withstood me twenty-one days; and behold, Michael, one of the chief princes, came to help me, for I had been left alone there with the kings of Persia. Now I have come to make you understand what will happen to your people in the latter days, for the vision refers to many days yet to come."

God heard Daniel the minute he prayed and dispatched His angel with the answer, all because of Daniel's words. The delay was due to warfare in the high places, but Michael came to assure that the answer got through to Daniel.

The angel goes on to say:

> And now I must return to fight with the prince of Persia; and when I have gone forth, indeed the prince of Greece will come. But I will tell you what is noted in the Scripture of Truth. No one upholds me against these, except Michael, your prince.
>
> —Daniel 10:20–21

We know from Hebrews 1:14 that angels minister to the heirs of salvation, and we see from Daniel's experience that Michael was his prince. Does it follow that there is an assigned bond between certain people and/or nations and God's angels? Jesus said:

> Take heed that you do not despise one of these little ones, for I say to you that in heaven their angels always see the face of My Father who is in heaven.
> —MATTHEW 18:10

I don't know about you, but I have not outgrown my need for an angel who has full access to the Father on my behalf! In Psalm 91:11–13, we are told:

> For He shall give His angels charge over you, To keep you in all your ways. In their hands they shall bear you up, Lest you dash your foot against a stone. You shall tread upon the lion and the cobra, The young lion and the serpent [Satan] you shall trample underfoot.

A few months ago I was driving in the morning to my volunteer job as a prayer counselor. I was at a point where I had topped the hill and was proceeding down into the valley. It was a dull, overcast day and the sun was doing its best to break through, like a gray circle in the sky with a rim of silver. Stretched across the horizon was a straight ribbon of gold, silver, and pure white light. The sight took my breath away, and then the words of an old hymn poured out of me:

## THERE'S A LIGHT SHINING FORTH

There's a light shining forth,
I can see it on the horizon.
It's the army of God, preparing for war.

Coming conquering, victorious
O'er the army of Satan,
Nothing shall stand before the army of God![4]

And then I cried, "Lord Jesus, are You coming soon?"
And He said, "Yes! Yes!"

I drove on to my destination, exhilarated, and that morning I was privileged to pray with two clients. The first was James, who to my amazement had never heard of the Holy Spirit; James also had a pinched nerve in his shoulder and could not raise his arm. I share the scriptures about the Holy Spirit and His work in our lives to equip and point us to Jesus. James surrendered all of himself to be indwelt by the Holy Spirit; the Holy Spirit graciously came into James' heart and also healed his shoulder. His arm shot straight up and he could not contain his joy!

The other client was Paul, who was depressed because of lack of work, feeling he was a failure. He had been filled with the Holy Spirit but needed a fresh touch. He also had severe back pain, which limited his ability to work. As we prayed, the spirit of heaviness fled and Paul was filled with laughter; his back was healed, leaving him free of all pain! That was a hallelujah morning!

I had other appointments that afternoon at nearby Christian City Convalescent Center. In the lobby I ran into the caregiver for a friend of mine, whom I was going to visit. He was sharing my friend's condition, and I said I knew he was depressed and I would go spread some cheer. It happened that an elderly man was walking by and he overheard my remarks. I proceeded to the elevator and the man got on with me. He asked if I were a counselor, and I replied that while I had a master's degree, I was not licensed but just tried to help people as a ministry. He then told me that he had a master's degree in Old Testament theology and I said how exciting that was. He continued: "I don't say this to everybody because they'll think I'm crazy, but do you know that Jesus is coming again soon?" I replied: "Let me tell you what I saw this morning!!!"

Daniel prepared himself to receive God's answer to his prayer by setting his heart to understand and humbling himself. Doesn't it just make common sense that we, as God's New Testament children with Christ living in us through the power of the Holy Spirit, put on daily the *whole* armor of God—not only in obedience to His word, but also to prepare ourselves to receive His answers to our prayers and to "co-operate" with our angels? The battle is intensifying as we draw nearer to the end, and we cannot afford any exposed weak spots. If you give the enemy an inch, he will take a mile! Show him and his demons no mercy, and pray without ceasing (1 Thess. 5:17)!

We may know the importance of the whole armor of God but often forget that we are in a war. Sometimes we goof up, and that happened to me just recently. A pastor friend of mine calls these slips the "oops" sins. They are not intentional; they just happen because God isn't finished with us yet; we are still under construction. But we can take heart, for He is coming soon!

## Oops!

I forgot to put on my full armor today,
And the enemy came—stole my peace away.
It was a very subtle attack,
Just a few words, then WHACK!

It was to be a casual conversation with my friend,
But our views clashed and harmony hit a dead-end.

Lord, what was the lesson to be learned by this
    wreck?
That love is more important than being correct!

AND, always start your day fully dressed,
The whole armor of God resists distress!

Consider these twelve keys that work together in prayer:

1. **The Name of Jesus.** "And whatever you
   ask in My name, that I will do, that the
   Father may be glorified in the Son. If you
   ask anything in My name, I will do it"
   (John 14:13–14).

2. **The Holy Spirit**. "Likewise the Spirit
   also helps in our weaknesses. For we do
   not know what we should pray for as
   we ought, but the Spirit Himself makes
   intercession for us with groanings which
   cannot be uttered" (Rom. 8:26).

3. **The Word/God's Will**. "Now this is the
   confidence that we have in Him, that if
   we ask anything according to His will, He
   hears us. And if we know that He hears
   us, whatever we ask, we know that we
   have the petitions that we have asked of
   Him" (1 John 5:14–15).

4. **Faith and Faith-Filled Words**. "So Jesus
   answered and said to them, 'Have faith in
   God. For assuredly, I say to you, whoever
   says to this mountain, "Be removed and
   cast into the sea," and does not doubt in

his heart, but believes that those things he says will be done, he will have whatever he says. Therefore, I say to you, whatever things you ask when you pray, believe that you receive them, and you will have them'" (Mark 11:22–26).

5. **Obedience**. "Therefore, I exhort first of all that supplications, prayers, intercessions, and giving of thanks be made for all men…for this is good and acceptable in the sight of God our Savior" (1 Tim. 2:1, 3).

6. **Perseverance**. Jesus tells of the friend coming at midnight, knocking on the door and asking for bread. He concludes: "I say to you, though he will not rise and give to him because he is his friend, yet because of his persistence he will rise and give him as many as he needs" (Luke 11:8).

7. **Purity of Heart/Righteousness**. "The effective, fervent prayer of a righteous man avails much" (James 5:16).

8. **Forgiveness**. "Therefore, if you bring your gift to the altar, and there remember that your brother has something against you, leave your gift there before the altar, and go your way. First be reconciled to your brother, and then come and offer your gift" (Matt. 5:23–24).

9. **Binding and Loosing**. "And I will give you the keys of the kingdom of heaven,

and whatever you bind on earth will be bound in heaven, and whatever you loose on earth will be loosed in heaven" (Matt. 16:19).

10. **Fasting and Prayer** (twin guns). "However, this kind does not go out except by prayer and fasting" (Matt. 17:21).

We have previously covered (11) **Asking**, and (12) **Abiding**. Perhaps even more keys come to your mind; but suffice it to say, we have all we need to be "more than conquerors" (Rom. 8:37).

But there is one more thing, a baker's dozen; and I confess it brings me joy. Pastor Jentezen Franklin has a weekly television program that I try not to miss because he is a teacher of the Word. The Holy Spirit is so precious to put teachings in your path at just the right time. I was in the middle of writing this chapter and Franklin was teaching on demonic forces that are attacking the saints; he spoke on the whole armor of God. He further said that if we wanted to drive Satan crazy, we just (13) **plead the blood of Jesus**! We are overcomers "by the blood of the Lamb and by the word of [our] testimony" (Rev. 12:11).

The last night of the Israelites' enslavement in Egypt, prior to their departure the following morning for the Promised Land, Moses called for all the elders and gave them specific instructions:

> Pick out and take lambs for yourselves according to your families, and kill the Passover lamb. And you shall take a bunch of hyssop, dip it in the blood that is in the basin, and strike the lintel and the two doorposts with the blood that is in the basin. And none

of you shall go out of the door of his house until morning. For the Lord will pass through to strike the Egyptians; and when He sees the blood on the lintel and on the two doorposts, the Lord will pass over the door and not allow the destroyer to come into your houses to strike you.

—Exodus 12:21–23

The Passover Lamb is our Lord Jesus Christ, the lintel and the two doorposts represent the cross, and the blood is His blood shed for us for the remission of sins. As believers in Christ, we have been washed in the blood; therefore, the destroyer cannot lawfully come into our houses to strike us. Our part is to "plead the blood" over our minds, souls, and bodies and over our faith, families, and futures and over our nation and states and over the church. We draw that blood line in the sand and the enemy cannot cross over. It does drive him crazy! Praise the Lord!

A friend sent me the following post on Facebook:

> I want to be so full of Jesus that if a mosquito bites me, it flies away singing, "There's Power in the Blood!"

Yes, Praise the Lord, because Satan hates our praise as well. God inhabits (makes His dwelling) in the praise of His people (Ps. 22:3, KJV). I don't think it is coincidence that this particular verse is in Psalm 22, which speaks also of the suffering of the Messiah.

Don't you know Satan kicks himself when he thinks of Paul and Silas in the jail cell at midnight, the darkest it could be, praising the Lord? He should have kept them separated, because one can "chase a thousand, And two can put ten thousand to flight" (Deut. 32:30). There was a great earthquake, the foundations were shaken, all doors opened, and everyone's chains loosed. Then the jailer and his entire family accepted Christ and were baptized (Acts 16:25–34).

After Paul's instructions on the whole armor of God, he concludes with this request in Ephesians 6:18–20:

> Praying always with all prayer and supplication in the Spirit, being watchful to this end with all perseverance and supplication for all the saints—and for me, that utterance may be given to me, that I may open my mouth boldly to make known the mystery of the gospel, for which I am an ambassador in chains; that in it I may speak boldly, as I ought to speak.

We know that Paul was personally called by Jesus Christ on the Damascus Road (see Acts 9:1–18), that he was a great missionary who established many churches, and that he wrote over half of the New Testament. His plea to the saints was that they pray "always," for their prayers played a major role in the success of his mission. He needed to speak with clarity and with boldness, his words to reveal the "mystery of the gospel."

How often do people ask us to pray for them and we nod our heads in agreement, but then we forget? We should pray right then, at the time of their request, so that we can pray in agreement and they will know prayers have gone up and the blessings will surely come down, because God says so.

Looking back over my life, I tried to remember the first time I prayed. Probably it was in school when I wanted to make a good grade on a test. My childhood was basically uneventful, no tragedies or traumas, except for the time we were tested for tuberculosis in the sixth grade and I was scheduled for a repeat test. I was very frightened but did not tell anyone. I rode my bike every day for exercise and ate a lot of apples. The results of the second test showed that

I had some scar tissue on my lungs as the result of pneumonia when I was a baby. What a relief!

I have a special place in my heart for Hannah in the Old Testament, because I also had difficulty in conceiving a child and could relate to her anguish. In 1 Samuel 1:15 she is praying in the temple. Priest Eli assumes that she is drunk because she was speaking in her heart, not out loud. She answers her accuser, saying:

> No, my lord, I am a woman of sorrowful spirit. I have drunk neither wine nor intoxicating drink, but have poured out my soul before the Lord.

Eli then agrees with her prayer (v. 17), saying:

> Go in peace, and the God of Israel grant your petition which you have asked of Him.

Faith arises in Hannah, "and her face was no longer sad" (v. 18) because she knows in her heart that her answer is coming. And indeed, about that time next year she "bore a son, and called his name Samuel, saying, 'Because I have asked for him from the LORD'" (v. 20).

I had been married seven years when I bore a son, Steven. I had promised the Lord he would be named after the first Christian martyr, Stephen. I thought perhaps I had erred in spelling his name with a "V" but the Lord assured me that the "V" was for victory, and the spelling was fine with Him. Like Hannah, I was blessed to later bear another son and a daughter. My cup runneth over!

I have prayed for years for the mates of God's choosing who were "out there somewhere" and who would enter my children's (and now grandchildren's) lives at just the right time. There was another mother praying as well, and one day her son met my daughter.

## Two Praying Mothers

"There's this guy," said this daughter of mine,
And I knew Love had arrived—right on time.
After all, I had prayed for her mate,
This was no coincidence—no "hand of fate."

Our Lord had arranged this intricate plan,
Putting him in the choir—a bass-singing man,
And she was the choir leader—beautiful and bright.
Romance was birthed in the music that night.

"There's this girl," said the son to his mother.
She, too, had prayed—there could be no other.
Stacey and Russell—just meant to be.
Two mothers…to God…blessings for eternity.

# Chapter 15
## PROTECTION

**D**AVID WAS THE greatest of the kings of Israel. He was a shepherd, a worshiper, and a psalmist. He was the devoted and loyal friend of Jonathan, the son of King Saul. The Lord called David a man after His own heart (Acts 13:22), and made a covenant with David that from his descendants would come the Messiah, and that David's throne would be everlasting (2 Sam. 7:16; Acts 13:23).

The first king, Saul, had fallen from God's grace. Samuel was instructed to go to Jesse of Bethlehem to anoint one of his sons as Saul's successor. The Lord rejected the first seven, but when David was brought before Samuel, the Lord said:

> "Arise, anoint him; for this is the one!" Then Samuel took the horn of oil and anointed him in the midst of his brothers; and the Spirit of the Lord came upon David from that day forward.
> —1 SAMUEL 16:12–13

Let's return to 1 Samuel 17, the story of David versus Goliath, for a different slant. When the Israelite soldiers are afraid to fight, David steps forward. King Saul then questions his ability, because he is just a youth (v. 33). David assures the king that just as he had killed the lion and the bear while tending his father's sheep, he would prevail against this "uncircumcised Philistine" as well, because he has "defied the armies of the living God" (vv. 36–37). David fells the giant with just one stone from his slingshot and then he cut off Goliath's head with his own sword, at which point the Israelites chased and defeated the Philistines (vv. 49–51).

Saul thereafter sets David over the men of war, and he found favor with all the people and Saul's servants (18:5). Returning home after a battle, the women were dancing and singing: "Saul has slain his thousands, And David his tens of thousands" (vv. 6–7). This angered Saul and from that day forward he "eyed David" (vv. 8–9).

Over a period of four years, on approximately twenty-one occasions, Saul seeks to kill David. David knows that he has been chosen to be the next king, but he honors Saul as his king. On several occasions David could have killed Saul but he refuses to do so, because God's Word says: "Do not touch My anointed ones, And do My prophets no harm" (1 Chron. 16:22).

This period of time is often referred to as David's "cave days," because he runs to the Wilderness of En Gedi and hides in caves. David was going through that "Dark Night of the Soul," which Saint John of the Cross wrote about in his classic poem of that name.[1] "The main idea can be seen as the painful experience that people endure as they seek to grow in spiritual maturity and union with God."[2] The Lord was preparing David to be king; he was going through boot camp.

David escaped to the cave of Adullam, and his family went to him:

> And everyone who was in distress, everyone who was in debt, and everyone who was discontented gathered to him. So he became captain over them. And there were four hundred men with him.
> —1 Samuel 22:2

151

This was a ragtag bunch, but they are later referred to as "mighty men of valor" (1 Chron. 12:21) and they accomplished mighty exploits. For instance, Adino the Eznite killed eight hundred men at one time; Eleazar fought against the Philistines so long and hard that his hand stuck to the sword; Shammah fought in the bean field and killed the Philistines (2 Sam. 23:8–12). Abishai killed three hundred men with a spear (v. 18), and Benaiah killed a lion in the middle of a pit on a snowy day, and he took a spear away from an Egyptian and killed him with it (vv. 20–22). They were loyal to David, their leader.

David is a mighty warrior and captain over mighty men, so who does he run to for protection? Who is mightier than he; who has the power and the resources to deliver him? David wrote many psalms during the dark nights of his soul, those "cave days," and we will find our answer there.

Psalm 57, written when David fled from Saul into the cave, verses 1–3:

> Be merciful to me, O God, be merciful to me! For my soul trusts in You; And in the shadow of Your wings I will make my refuge, Until these calamities have passed by. I will cry out to God Most High, To God who performs all things for me. He shall send from heaven and save me; He reproaches the one who would swallow me up. Selah God shall send forth His mercy and His truth.

Psalm 142 is a prayer of David when he was in the cave (vv. 1–2, 5):

> I cry out to the LORD with my voice; With my voice I make my supplication; I pour out my complaint before Him; I declare before Him my trouble... I

cried out to You, O LORD; I said, "You are my refuge;
My portion in the land of the living."

Psalm 3 was written in that "dark night" when David
fled from Absalom, his son:

> LORD, how they have increased who trouble me!
> Many are they who rise up against me. Many are they
> who say of me, "There is no help for him in God." But
> You, O LORD, are a shield for me, my glory and the
> One who lifts up my head. I cried to the LORD with
> my voice, And He heard me from His holy hill. I lay
> down and slept; I awoke, for the LORD sustained me.
> I will not be afraid of ten thousands of people Who
> have set themselves against me all around.
> —PSALM 3:1–6

Psalm 18 in the *Christian Life Bible* (NKJV) is captioned:
"God the Sovereign Savior. To the Chief Musician. A Psalm
of David the servant of the Lord, who spoke to the Lord
the words of this song on the day that the Lord delivered
him from the hand of all his enemies and from the hand of
Saul."[3] David said:

> I will love You, O LORD, my strength. The LORD is
> my rock and my fortress and my deliverer; My God,
> my strength, in whom I will trust; My shield and
> the horn of my salvation, my stronghold. I will call
> upon the LORD, who is worthy to be praised; So shall
> I be saved from my enemies. The pangs of death sur-
> rounded me, and the floods of ungodliness made me
> afraid…In my distress I called upon the LORD, and
> cried out to my God…He bowed the heavens also
> and came down…The LORD thundered from heaven,
> And the Most High uttered His voice…He sent from

above, He took me; He drew me out of many waters; He delivered me from my strong enemy, From those who hated me, For they were too strong for me…But the LORD was my support. He also brought me out into a broad place; He delivered me because He delighted in me…For by You I can run against a troop, By my God I can leap over a wall. As for God, His way is perfect; The word of the LORD is proven. He is a shield to all who trust in Him…The LORD lives! Blessed be my Rock! Let the God of my salvation be exalted. It is God who avenges me, And subdues the peoples under me; He delivers me from my enemies…You have delivered me from the violent man. Therefore, I will give thanks to You, O LORD, among the Gentiles, And sing praises to Your name. Great deliverance He gives to His king, And shows mercy to His anointed, To David and his descendants forevermore.

—PSALM 18:1–4, 6, 9, 13, 16–19, 29–30, 46–50

The story is told of a young woman in dire straits who came to an older woman of great faith seeking a solution to her many problems. The young woman set forth her issue, and the woman of faith replied, "But God." The younger replies, "You don't understand," and then she would recite her calamity. The woman of faith would again reply, "But God." Again and again the younger woman complains, but the reply is the same, "But God." The woman of faith goes on to say, "When you have God, you have all you need or can possibly desire."

# HE COMES!

There are days when problems mount up,
Too innumerable to count.
Like raging waves in the ocean they come,
One on top of the other.
Is there ever an end?

And then I run to my Father
And cry for help, in the Name of the Son,
Faithfully He comes in the Power of His Spirit,
And speaks to the waves, as in days of old,
"Peace, be still!"

And the problems, so overwhelming and
    insurmountable,
Become as tiny ripples in a calm sea.
Once more He has shown His faithfulness—
All is well with my soul!

David's *protection* is *provided* through the *power* of the Almighty Lord. That's a lot of "P's!" and we know that David *prayed*, another "P" that we previously covered in chapter 14. However, there is a type of prayer which fits in this category of "protection," and I purposely wanted to include it here. Since I am the author, I am sure you will allow me this latitude. I'm talking about intercessory prayer.

I have heard it said that intercessory prayer means that the pray-er virtually takes the position of the pray-ee, personally experiencing the pain, distress, and emotions of the pray-ee. I believe this is true to an extent because of my personal experiences, but there is more to intercessory prayer than that.

Dutch Sheets wrote the best book I have ever read on

this subject. It is appropriately entitled *Intercessory Prayer: How God Can Use Your Prayers to Move Heaven and Earth*. He relates an incident from a mission in a remote village in Guatemala. A little girl, six or seven years old, was tied to a tree because she was insane and could not be controlled. The Lord told Sheets to pray for her "in the name of this Jesus you've been preaching about." Evil powers would be broken and they "can believe that the Jesus you are preaching about is who you say He is." He was to be His spokesman and release what Jesus had already done; and so he prayed, the little girl was set free, and the village turned to Christ.[4]

Sheets continues:

> And a new plan unfolded to me. A new concept emerged—Jesus and me. For the first time I understood the heavenly pattern: Jesus is the Victor—we're the enforcers; Jesus is the Redeemer—we're the releasers; Jesus is the head—we are the Body...So the partnership goes on—God and humans. But the correct pattern is critical: My prayers of intercession release Christ's finished work of intercession.
>
> His work empowers my prayers—my prayers release His work. Mine extends His—His effectuates mine. Mine activates His—His validates mine. In Kingdom Enterprises we're not in the production department. We're in distribution...BIG difference. He's the generator. We're the distributors. I think this makes us His co-laborers. What do you think? I think Christ is awesome and wants us to be "awesomites."...More than conquerors! Christ and His Christ-ians, changing things on the earth.[5]

Is this not what Jesus said when He gave the Great Commission, telling us to "Go, *therefore*" (Matt. 28:19, emphasis added)? What is the "therefore" there for? It's because He has *all* authority "in heaven and on earth" (v. 18, emphasis added). He has extended this authority to His followers, and we are to "re-present" Him here on earth. He said we would do even greater works than He did while He was on earth. How is that possible? It's simply because Jesus was limited to one human body; now He is multiplied through His disciples. Instead of one Jesus, there are now "zillions" of His sent ones.

> Most assuredly, I say to you, he who believes in Me, the works that I do he will do also; and greater works than these he will do, because I go to My Father. And whatever you ask in My name, that I will do, that the Father may be glorified in the Son. If you ask anything in My name, I will do it.
>
> —JOHN 14:12–14

A little girl was crying one night after her mother had tucked her in for the night. Her little brother came to her side and asked what was wrong. She was afraid, thinking there was something under the bed. He looked and assured her it was all clear; there was nothing to fear and Jesus was with her. She replied, "I need somebody with skin on!" We are to be "Jesus-with-skin-on" to our world.

We have an added bonus in addition to the authority and name of Jesus. He has sent to us "another Helper" and He abides with us forever (John 14:16). Just prior to His ascension, the followers of Jesus were instructed to wait in Jerusalem for this Promise of the Father, the Holy Spirit (Acts 1:4), and on the day of Pentecost, He came to empower them to be witnesses for Jesus.

> And they were all filled with the Holy Spirit and
> began to speak with other tongues as the Spirit gave
> them utterance.
>
> —ACTS 2:4

And we read how Peter, who had denied Jesus three times and had gone back to fishing, went into the streets of Jerusalem preaching the good news and "three thousand souls were added to them" (Acts 2:41). The remainder of the New Testament testifies of the followers of Jesus moving in the power of the Holy Spirit to continue His work. We "co-operate" with the Holy Spirit.

Paul speaks of travailing when he writes to the Galatians:

> My little children, of whom I travail in birth again
> until Christ be formed in you.
>
> —GALATIANS 4:19, KJV

He had travailed first for them to come to Christ, and now he is travailing again because they seem to be falling back into the bondage of the law. This travail means the pangs of childbirth; he is interceding in prayer for Christ to be formed in them, much like a mother travails to bring her baby to birth.

When my husband Bob left, there were many occasions when I would be called to travail for his salvation. I would sit in my rocking chair, praying so hard that my knuckles would turn white as I clinched to the arms of the chair. I prayed until my peace returned, and then I would thank and praise the Lord for working in his life. Bob left in June 1978; in October 2004 I had the pleasure of praying personally with Bob as he affirmed his faith in Christ as his Lord and Savior.

We must never stop interceding until our victory is

manifested, or our *knower knows* that all is well, because many times we will not know who we are praying for—just that we are to pray in obedience to His call.

I find also that I am called to intercede for Jerusalem. The burden just falls on me and I find myself weeping, just as Jesus did when He looked out over the city:

> O Jerusalem, Jerusalem, the one who kills the prophets and stones those who are sent to her! How often I wanted to gather your children together, as a hen gathers her brood under her wings, but you were not willing!
>
> —LUKE 13:34

David wrote:

> Pray for the peace of Jerusalem: "May they prosper who love you. Peace be within your walls, Prosperity within your palaces." For the sake of my brethren and companions, I will now say, "Peace be within you." Because of the house of the LORD our God I will seek your good.
>
> —PSALM 122:6–9

On my second trip to Israel in 1997, I was blessed to have a conversation with Jan Willem van der Hoeven of the International Christian Embassy. He said that the reason Jerusalem is so important is because the Temple Mount will be the site of the third temple. He said Yeshua did not come to start a new religion; but when we become believers, we become Jews. I asked him why I had that strange feeling of being home in Israel, and he shared about being engrafted into the one tree (see Romans 11:1–27). He went on to say that each person receives a call, either come home to Israel or be an intercessor. He told me that I was an intercessor.

Our Lord Jesus wept over Jerusalem, and "He always lives to make intercession" as our High Priest (Heb. 7:25). Does it not follow that we as His followers are to intercede as well until He comes again to rule and reign in the New Jerusalem (Rev. 21–22)? We must be about our Father's business, just like Jesus.

My daughter had gone to Sweden to visit the family that hosted her when she was an exchange student. They were encouraging her to stay, not return home on schedule. She was torn between her two families. The Lord called me to pray the evening before her departure, and I could sense her confusion. I went to my knees in intercession for my daughter and "prayed through." Coming home from the airport the following evening, she said I would never know the struggle she had under all the pressure to stay. I was able to reply, "Oh, yes I do!"

There was another particular time in my life when I could feel the power of prayer; it was tangible! My husband's attorney wanted to take my deposition in his divorce case. I worked for lawyers and knew full well what a deposition was—you give your testimony in the lawyer's office instead of before the court. Still, this was very upsetting to me because I was still convinced our marriage would one day be restored; so why all this testimony, all this talking in vain? A group of friends in church were praying for me; and as I was about to arrive at the lawyer's office, I could feel my spirit inside being lifted up. All nervousness and fear were gone; I was at perfect peace. My attorney met with me first and shared how Bob's attorney believed his client was making a big mistake. During the deposition he was most gracious, and I wondered why he was asking certain questions, as the answers favored me, not Bob. It was a most cordial deposition because it was undergirded in prayer.

My sister-in-law Barbara asked that I pray for a young man who had a college scholarship for football and was all set to go when he was struck with leukemia, the fast moving strain. I could not stop thinking of Brian and was praying for him constantly. One day I deliberately reached out and touched the hem of Jesus' garment on behalf of Brian, and then I got my "good feeling" and knew he was healed. Thank You, Jesus! Barbara called that evening, so excited. "You'll never guess what happened!" I told her I knew he was healed. Yes!

The Lord told me that He has a network. When there is a need, He calls on certain saints to pray. We must stay on the alert, for the enemy prowls around "like a roaring lion, seeking whom he may devour" (1 Pet. 5:8). Note that he is not a lion, he just roars to put fear in your heart so you will forget who you are and the authority you have to put him under your feet.

Dan, a missionary friend of mine, tells the story of a village being attacked by a killer lion. The people sent for two missionary brothers to come to their aid. They went out into the tall grasses with their rifles and slowly walked forward, back to back. When the lion attacked, one brother shot and killed the lion, protecting the other brother. He had his back. As Christians, we have each other's back.

## SOUND THE ALARM!

Heaven to Earth: Sound the Alarm!
Christian Soldiers: To the front of the line!
Satan and his demons are set on harm,
Seeking to destroy these children of Mine.

Wield the weapons in your hand,
Plead the Blood, pray in His Name,
On the Word of God firmly stand,
Banish devils to the pit whence they came!

Jesus paid full price on the cross
To set the captives free.
This battle the enemy has lost,
My children shout in victory!

The Greater One Lives in Me!

# Chapter 16
## PERSEVERANCE

W HEN WE ARE trying to lose weight and get in shape, there is a saying: "no pain, no gain." If we do not put forth that extra effort, deny self, and do some sweating, we will not achieve our goal. We must persevere concerning not just our physical body, but our spiritual man as well.

In the Book of James, we are told to

> Consider it a sheer gift...when tests and challenges come at you from all sides. You know that under pressure, your faith-life is forced into the open and shows its true colors. So don't try to get out of anything prematurely. Let it do its work so you become mature and well-developed, not deficient in any way.
> —JAMES 1:2–5, THE MESSAGE

A friend recently said to me, "I'm too blessed to be stressed," and, of course, I laughed. But a certain amount of stress is not a bad thing. Consider this:

> A Diamond Is Merely a Lump of Coal That Did Well Under Pressure...It's a very powerful image, expressed succinctly and beautifully...diamonds... beautiful, light defracting gems that do more than sparkle, they create optical magic...coal...dirty, product of decaying plants, pollutant. Apply pressure to coal, WOW, extraordinary transformation. Who wouldn't

want to be transformed from coal to diamond? Someone who's afraid of hard work, that's who![1]

Isn't that what our Lord's up to with us? He wants to transform us into the "image of His Son" (Rom. 8:29).

"They shall be Mine," says the LORD of hosts, "On the day I make them My jewels."
—MALACHI 3:17

Peter reminds us how fortunate we are, as believers, to have

...a future in heaven—and that future starts now! God is keeping careful watch over us and the future. The Day is coming when you will have it all—life healed and whole...even though you have to put up with every kind of aggravation in the meantime. Pure gold put in the fire comes out of it *proved* pure; genuine faith put through this suffering comes out *proved* genuine. When Jesus wraps it all up, it's your faith, not your gold, that God will have on display as evidence of His victory.
—1 PETER 1:4–7, THE MESSAGE, EMPHASIS ADDED

I remember as a little girl going to my Grandpa's farm and watching my Grandma wash clothes in a big black wash pot in the yard. She would put the clothes and soap in the pot of water with a small fire underneath, and then she would keep adding logs to get the water hotter and hotter, stirring the clothes with a big wooden paddle to get the dirt out and the clothes clean. That's what our Lord does with our faith. He puts it in a pot and keeps turning up the heat to burn off the dross until He can look into the pot and see His own reflection. Our refined faith is His trophy. Isn't it amazing how much a trophy looks like a wash pot on a pedestal?

Even though we have read our Bibles and know that the tests will come, isn't our initial reaction when trials do come to say, "This can't be happening to me! Surely the Lord doesn't know what I'm going through. If He did, He'd be doing something about it"? I confess that right after my husband left and I was so crushed, I went out into my backyard, put my fist up in the air and cried, "God, why aren't You doing something about this?" He was.

Did not the Captain of our faith also go through some "aggravation," to put it mildly? Jesus was made "perfect" in His sufferings (Heb. 5:8–9); so are we. He calls us to perfection, or maturity, saying:

> Therefore you shall be perfect, just as Your Father in heaven is perfect.
> —MATTHEW 5:48

Jesus warned us in advance that we would have obstacles to face, saying:

> In the world you will have tribulation; but be of good cheer, I have overcome the world.
> —JOHN 16:33

Because Jesus overcame, we can be confident that we shall overcome as well "because as He is, so are we in this world" (1 John 4:17). That is present tense, meaning right now, we are overcomers "by the blood of the Lamb and the word of [our] testimony" (Rev. 12:11). There is no testimony without a test, no message without a mess, and no overcoming without something to overcome.

The test you go through is not just for God to give you a

grade but for you to see your progress report. Perhaps there are some areas in your character that need a bit of refining; perhaps some sharp edges need to be honed through the sandpaper of adversity. In Proverbs 27:17, we read that "iron sharpens iron." Are there people in your life who rub you the wrong way and many times you feel you are butting heads, like two bulls?

I had an appointment with a certain lady; and I knew beforehand that the meeting could get a little testy, so I prayed intensely, being certain I had on the whole armor of God. All was going well, but then a remark hit my Achilles heel and my whole armor fell down around my knees. Angry words spewed out of my mouth, much to my surprise and chagrin. I felt exposed as a hypocrite, and I wanted to run home and hide in my cave, like David. But, like David, I had to get up and get going again. Satan loves it when we sit out the game, feeding on his platter of condemnation when all we need to do is ask for forgiveness, receive it as done, and continue to walk in love. It's not how many times you fall down, but how many times you get up and start all over again—this is perseverance.

David writes in Psalm 23, the shepherd's psalm:

> *Yea*, though I *walk* through the valley…I will fear no evil, for You are with me.
> —PSALM 23:4, EMPHASIS ADDED

Note that it is certain; it is *yea*, not *maybe*. There will be valleys; you can count on it, but you can also count on Him walking with you. Our Lord is for us, never against us.

And it is to *walk* (no running here). We don't mature overnight. It is a process and it takes time. We are such "instant" people—instant coffee, instant mashed potatoes.

Another post I received from a friend on Facebook said, "God wants Crock-Pot faith, not microwave!"

*Through the valley*: We come through; we don't stay in the valley. We are just passing through, developing some faith muscles on our way. We are coming through like shining gold because of our Lord's purpose.

*I will fear no evil*: The battle is won in the mind, not the emotions. We make the decision, the determination not to fear. We say, "I will not fear!" as an act of our will. Jesus conquered for us in the Garden of Gethsemane when He prayed, "Nevertheless, not as I will, but as You will" (Matt. 26:39). God's will for us is *never the less* but *always the more*. We can confidently pray, "Thy will be done" (6:10), because His will is the best for His children.

We long for the easy, yellow brick road, but there is no such thing in our walk with Christ. The way to victory is through perseverance.

The definition of *perseverance* in Webster's is to persist, remaining steadfast to a purpose, idea or task in face of difficulties. It is to be patient. I'm reminded of the prayer for patience: "Lord, I want patience and I want it NOW!

Still you say, "God made me a promise; I know it was His voice. He even confirmed it to me." Well, keep standing on that promise—*persevere*! Joy does come in *the* morning (Ps. 30:5). We just are not sure which morning that will be, but we can rest assured our deliverance will come in the fullness of God's time. He does make *all* things beautiful in *His* time (Eccl. 3:11). (No half-baked potatoes for His kids.) Plus, we have the promise that "*every detail* in our lives of love for God is worked into something good" (Rom. 8:28, THE MESSAGE, emphasis added).

I have found that the victory is especially sweet when we have waited a long time. I have previously shared this testimony, but it was such a pivotal point in my life when my husband left. There was such a sharp contrast between the day of his departure—when I felt the wind, the waves, and the water coming over me, pushing me down, down— and the point in time of love and restoration—when I was carried to the mountaintop of pure love. Thirty years earlier I was as low as I could get and still survive; and on this day of fulfillment, I was as high as I could get and still survive.

There is an interesting concept that Bill Gothard teaches in his Institute of Basic Youth Conflict seminars. God will give you a dream or a vision for your life, but then con- trary circumstances arise and it appears that the vision has died. As you persevere and hold fast to your vision, God is developing your character, and when He deems the timing is right, He supernaturally fulfills your vision.

For example, Abraham had a promise from God that he would be the father of a great nation and have so many descendants that they could not be numbered (Gen. 12:2–3; 13:15–16). The vision appeared to die when Sarah became too old to bear children. The vision was supernaturally fulfilled when God gave them a son in their old age, Isaac (20:2), who became the father of Jacob and Esau (25:19–26). Jacob, called Israel (35:10), which means "prince of God," was the father of twelve sons (vv. 22–26), the twelve tribes of Israel, the Jews. Esau was the father of the Edomites (36:43), known today as the Arabs. Could we begin to count Abraham's descendants?

Moses was given the vision of leading his people out of the bondage of Egypt (Exod. 3:7–12). God gave Moses power to perform signs and wonders, including the ten plagues, to convince Pharaoh and confirm to the Jews as well that God had chosen him to lead the nation to the Promised Land (see Exodus 3:13–20). Do you remember when Pharaoh asked Moses to remove the frogs, and Moses said, "O.K.—when?" Pharaoh replies, "Tomorrow" (8:10). He put up with frogs another whole day! He, too, was trying to persevere, but against God. Pharaoh at last insists that the people leave, and the Egyptians even financed their journey—back pay (12:31, 35–36).

They remain in the wilderness for forty years because of their unbelief (Num. 14:33–34). And when at last they are about to enter the Promised Land, Moses is forbidden to enter with them because of his rebellion in the desert of Zin when he disobeyed the Lord's instructions by not "speaking" to the rock, but instead "striking" it (20:7–12). He is able to view the Promised Land from the mountaintop but that was as far as he was to go at that time (27:12–14). This seems a bit harsh, but this was not the end of the matter. Moses was with Jesus on the Mount of Transfiguration, along with Elijah (Luke 9:28–33). He did make it, and in such glorious company!

Consider Mary, the mother of Jesus. One eventful day, Gabriel, God's messenger angel, told her that she would be the mother of the Messiah. She was elated, though perplexed. She was engaged to be married to Joseph, and this could present a major problem, perhaps even her death by stoning (Luke 1:26–35). Joseph was obedient to the leading of the Lord and became the earthly father of our Lord Jesus Christ (Matt. 1:18–25). Mary was warned by Simeon in the temple that a sword would also pierce her heart (Luke 2:35), but she could not know what these words really meant. After all, her son was Messiah, the Son of God; He would rule and reign someday, and she would be by His side. So how did it come to this—the Cross? Her Son was crucified, dead, and buried (John 19:25–42). Her vision likewise, was dead and buried; *but* the third day He arose (1 Cor. 15:3–5)!

The promise was resurrected as God's plan unfolded, and is still unfolding as we await His return. Any moment now we will hear the trumpet announce His second coming—are we ready?

There is the "promise of a promise" in Ephesians 2:10:

> For we are His workmanship [*poiema*], created in Christ Jesus for good works, which God prepared beforehand that we should walk in them.

God's children are His "poems," His "poetry." Before we were born, God had a plan for our lives:

> For I know the thoughts that I think toward you, says the LORD, thoughts of peace and not of evil, to give you a future and a hope.
> —JEREMIAH 29:11

(Dear reader: I told you these were two of my favorites!)

We are not here on earth just to take up space; there are destinies to fulfill. Each has his or her own unique purpose, and God wants to reveal that purpose to us; hence, the "birth of a vision." We must know what that purpose is in order to strive toward it.

Satan will come to distract and discourage us; but as we remain focused on the fulfillment of our vision, we will persevere during what seems to be the "death of the vision." In His grace, He gives us signposts along the way—maybe a song or the sermon that's just for you, or a friend calls with an encouraging word, or, of course, rainbows and pennies and birds on telephone wires. Best of all is when you are reading your Bible and the Word lights up for you.

What really matters is what you do during the interval between the receipt of the promise and the delivery. That is where you are brought to maturity, walking "by faith, not by sight" (2 Cor. 5:7). Remember *Indiana Jones and the Last Crusade*, when Dr. Jones comes to this huge dark abyss with no way across? As he steps out into space, a bridge pops out under his feet and he walks across. Of course, he has read the script, but so have we—we've read the "scriptures." We're going to the other side, too.

Since God is far more concerned with our character than our comfort, He uses this time of "waiting" to develop certain Christ-like qualities in us, called "the fruit of the Spirit" (Gal. 5:22–23). It is our character that supports our destiny.

We can see the importance of perseverance in the lives of Abraham, Moses, Mary, and also our own lives in order to fulfill the vision we carry in our hearts. It is clear that "where there is no vision, the people perish" (Prov. 29:18, KJV); but how do you do it? Is there a "How to Persist" formula? I can only tell you what works for me.

**First, prayer**: This involves not only talking to God, but listening as well. The prophet Samuel said to the Lord, "Speak, for Your servant hears" (1 Sam. 3:10). Shhh! Be quiet and listen! It's hard to hear when you are talking. "Be still, and know that I am God" (Ps. 46:10).

**Second, Bible reading**: We must get into the Word, and the Word must get into us. Then, when we get bumped (and we will), the Word will spill out. There are a "zillion" precious promises to stand on. Jesus defeated Satan with the Word and we are to do the same.

**Third, fasting**: Fasting on a consistent basis keeps the flesh down and the spirit up. Sin entered the world when Eve took that first bite; and how often we sin with our mouths, the words we speak. Jesus said, "When you fast" (Matt. 6:16), not "*if*." Fasting should be our lifestyle. Proclaim the purpose of your fast before the Lord, and show Him that you are serious. He means more to you than food; you want to bring glory to His name and to be used to advance His kingdom. We had a member of our church who was seriously ill, and we fasted together every Thursday as a congregation for the healing of this one we loved. She is an overcomer today!

**Fourth, corporate worship**: The Lord tells us not to "forsake the assembling of ourselves together" (Heb. 10:25). As we gather together to worship, praise the Lord, and lift Him up, He lifts us up. Christianity is not a "Lone Ranger" religion; we are the family of God. One of Satan's greatest tactics is isolationism.

**Fifth, small group fellowship**: I am blessed to have a special group of ladies that I have been meeting with since 1987; they are sisters to me. Also, there is a visitation group from our church and we go out on Wednesday mornings. This is where I see "pure religion and undefiled" (James 1:27, KJV) as we go to the widows, widowers, and those who are hurting. I am a member of Prayer Force, eight prayer warriors. I know Satan hates when we come together dressed in our full armor and send him packing. I have the greatest Sunday school class in the world (I know, you thought you did!). I learn so much from their input. Also, there is a class of ladies who are studying "Women of the Word," and that gets to be very interesting, if you get my drift. If you are not in a small group, then start one.

When all else fails, you simply breathe in, breathe out, keep putting one foot in front of the other, and most important of all—*never, never, never quit!*

Isaiah 40:31 says:

> They that *wait* upon the LORD shall renew their
> strength, they shall mount up with wings as eagles,

they shall run and not be weary, they shall walk and
not faint.

—Isaiah 40:31, KJV, EMPHASIS ADDED

The "waiting" here is not just time wise. It is also in the
nature of ministering, like waiting on tables, taking orders,
and meeting needs. Our strength is renewed in our waiting.

The Lord is calling us to be eagles, not turkeys. When an
eagle sees the storm coming, he sets his wings and flies right
into the face of the storm, letting the winds carry him high
above it all. You get a better perspective there. Adversity
can carry you to the high places. He takes us "exceedingly
abundantly above all that we ask or think, *according to the
power that works in us*" (Eph. 3:20, emphasis added). That
power is the Holy Spirit! We are to "co-operate" and "co-
mission" with Him.

# I WONDER

Sometimes I wonder if I shall ever be
The woman of God He called me to be.
I fall so often, landing flat on my face,
And question why I'm even in the race.

I'm not called to quit—this I know—
And it's not whether I run fast or slow.
There's honor in being chosen to run at all,
In being wise enough to answer Christ's call.

He promised I would not run by myself,
The Holy Spirit along side would give me help.
There's a cloud of witnesses cheering me on,
And God's grace leads me safely home!

So even if I wonder and stumble, that's OK,
For Jesus never fails to light my way.
I shall win the prize of His high calling laid up for
    me,
And celebrate with all the saints our glorious
    victory!

# Chapter 17
# PRAISE

I N GEOMETRY WE are taught that the shortest distance between two points is a straight line. In the Christian walk, the shortest distance between the valley and victory is praise. God dwells in the praise of His people (Ps. 22:3), and His presence insures success.

In the life of Joseph, we see how he prospered in spite of circumstances. After his brothers sold him into slavery, he was purchased by Potiphar, captain of the Egyptian guard.

> The LORD was with Joseph... And his master saw that the LORD was with him, and that the LORD made all he did to prosper in his hand. So Joseph found favor in his sight, and served him. Then he made him overseer of his house, and all that he had he put under his authority... the LORD blessed the Egyptian's house for Joseph's sake; and the blessing of the LORD was on all that he had in the house and in the field.
> —GENESIS 39:2–5

All was well until Joseph refused advances made by Potiphar's wife, and he was thrown into prison.

> But the LORD was with Joseph and showed him mercy, and He gave him favor in the sight of the keeper of the prison. And the keeper of the prison committed to Joseph's hand all the prisoners who were in the prison; whatever they did there, it was his

doing…because the Lord was with him, and whatever he did, the LORD made it prosper.

—GENESIS 39:21–23

Joseph later correctly interpreted the dreams of the Pharaoh's butler and baker. The baker was killed and the butler restored to serve again. Even though Joseph had requested that the butler remember him and make mention of him to Pharaoh, the butler forgot (see Genesis 40).

Two full years passed and then Pharaoh had a dream that no one could interpret, whereupon the butler remembered Joseph; he was brought before the Pharaoh, who asked Joseph to interpret the dream (see Genesis 41:1–15).

So Joseph answered Pharaoh, saying, "It is not in me; God will give Pharaoh an answer of peace."

—GENESIS 41:16

Joseph foretells seven years of plenty, followed by seven years of famine, and advises Pharaoh to appoint a discerning and wise man to collect the produce of Egypt during the full years to hold in reserve and dispense during the seven lean years (vv. 25–36).

So the advice was good in the eyes of Pharaoh and in the eyes of all his servants. And Pharaoh said to his servants, "Can we find such a one as this, a man in whom is the Spirit of God?" Then the Pharaoh said to Joseph, "Inasmuch as God has shown you all this, there is no one as discerning and wise as you. You shall be over my house, and all my people shall be ruled according to your word; only in regard to the throne will I be greater than you."

—GENESIS 41:37–40

Joseph was thirty years old and was given as his wife Asenath, the daughter of the priest of On (v. 45). She bore him two sons:

> Joseph called the name of the firstborn Manasseh: "For God has made me forget all my toil and all my father's house." And the name of the second he called Ephraim: "For God has caused me to be fruitful in the land of my affliction."
> —GENESIS 41:51–52

Note how Joseph continually praises and honors God in every situation, never claiming any glory for himself.

> The seven years of plenty…ended, and the seven years of famine began…The famine was over all the face of the earth, and Joseph opened all the store-houses…And the famine became severe in the land of Egypt. So all countries came to Joseph in Egypt to buy grain.
> —GENESIS 41:53–54, 56–57

This included Canaan, where Joseph's father, Jacob, and his eleven brothers lived. Jacob sends ten of his sons to Egypt to buy food. When they appear before Joseph, they do not recognize him; but he knows them. He grants their request, with the stipulation that they return home and bring Benjamin, his younger brother, back to Egypt with them, at which time he will release Simeon, who was being held in hostage. Jacob refuses to send Benjamin but the situation becomes dire (see Genesis 42).

Judah assures Jacob that he will be the surety for Benjamin, and they will all come back safely from Egypt; Jacob, with heavy heart, agrees to send his youngest son (see Genesis 43). All the brothers appear before Joseph.

And Joseph said to his brothers, "Please come near to me."...Then he said: "I am Joseph, your brother, whom you sold into Egypt. But now, do not therefore be grieved or angry with yourselves because you sold me here; for God has sent me before you to preserve life...And God sent me here before you to preserve a posterity for you in the earth, and to save your lives by a great deliverance. So now it was not you who sent me here, but God, and He has made me a father to Pharaoh...and a ruler throughout the land of Egypt. Hurry and go up to my father, and say to him, 'Thus says your son Joseph: God has made me lord of all Egypt; come down to me; do not tarry.'"

—GENESIS 45:4–5, 7–9

The brothers return to Canaan with the astonishing good news that Joseph is alive and reigns in Egypt; Jacob and all the households are to go to Egypt, not only to survive, but to thrive. Jacob, now called Israel, stops at Beersheba to offer sacrifices to the God of Isaac, his father.

Then God spoke to Israel in the visions of the night, and said, "Jacob, Jacob!" And he said, "Here I am." So He said, "I am God, the God of your father; do not fear to go down to Egypt, for I will make of you a great nation there. I will go down with you to Egypt, and I will also surely bring you up again; and Joseph will put his hand on your eyes."

—GENESIS 46:2–4

Jacob's life exemplified praise, worship, and honor to God. And it is well said in the idiom: the apple does not fall far from the tree. Joseph followed in his father's footsteps, and his life of praise was a conduit to bring forth the covenant God made with Abraham to make of him and his descendants a great nation (Gen. 17:4).

Jacob had a much earlier experience with God that launched him into this life of praise. After he had incurred the wrath of his brother Esau, when he had schemed to rob Esau of his birthright (25:29–34) and later the blessing of Isaac, their father (27:1–29), he was on the run to Haran and his kinfolk there. He stopped at Bethel (House of God), and made for himself a pillow of stone to rest his head (28:11).

> Then he dreamed, and behold, a ladder was set up on the earth, and its top reached to heaven; and there the angels of God were ascending and descending on it. And behold, the LORD stood above it and said: "I am the LORD God of Abraham your father and the God of Isaac; the land on which you lie I will give to you and your descendants."
>
> —GENESIS 28:12–13

The Lord then confirmed the covenant He had made with Abraham, and Jacob's response was:

> How awesome is this place! This is none other than the House of God, and this is the gate of heaven!
>
> —GENESIS 28:17

Jacob then poured oil on the stone, making it an altar of worship (v. 18). The picture here is our praise going up the ladder, and the Father sending the angels down in response to minister to the heirs of salvation (Heb. 1:14). Praise goes up, and the blessings come down. We must continue to climb the ladder of praise in spite of our circumstances. Remember the children's song: "We are climbing Jacob's ladder…higher and higher!"

Merlin Carothers, in his book entitled *Prison to Praise*,

goes into much detail about the power of praise, and he writes about a vision he had concerning the ladder of praise.

> In Ephesians, chapters one and two, I found my vision described by Paul in slightly different words: "Blessed (Praised!) be the God and Father of our Lord Jesus Christ, who hath blessed us with all spiritual blessings in heavenly places with Christ;...He hath chosen us in him before the foundation of the world, that we should be holy and without blame...To the praise of the glory of his grace...that in...the fullness of times he might gather together in one all things in Christ...That we should be to the praise of his glory, who first trusted in Christ...that you may know...what is the greatness of his power to us-ward who believe, according to the working of his mighty power, which he wrought in Christ, when he raised Him from the dead and set him at his own right hand in the heavenly places. Far above all principality and power, and might, and dominion...And hath raised us up together, and made us sit together in heavenly places in Christ Jesus." Jesus Christ is raised above all the powers of darkness, and according to God's word, our rightful inheritance is right there **above** the darkness together in Christ. The ladder is praise!"[1]

Carothers further asserts:

> I have come to believe that the prayer of praise is the highest form of communication with God, and one that releases a great deal of power into our lives. Praising Him is not something we do because we feel good, rather it is an act of obedience. Often the prayer of praise is done in sheer teeth-gritting will-power; yet when we persist in it, somehow the power

of God is released into us and into the situation, first in a trickle perhaps, but later in a growing stream that finally floods us and washes away the old hurts and scars.[2]

Most Christians are familiar with the whole armor of God as set forth in Ephesians 6:10–18, but is the mighty weapon of praise neglected through ignorance? King Jehoshaphat of Judah is a prime example of victory through praise. His story is in 2 Chronicles 20:1–30. The armies of Ammon, Moab, and Mount Seir have formed a coalition and are poised to strike Judah. King Jehoshaphat and the people of Judah are terrified, so the King proclaimed a fast and sought the Lord. As he stands in the assembly of Judah and Jerusalem, he prays to God, reminding Him of His covenant with Abraham and the people of Israel, his descendants, that God Himself gave them the land, and of His promise of protection when they cry out in distress. In verses 12, 14–15, we read:

> "O our God, will You not judge them? For we have no power against this great multitude that is coming against us; nor do we know what to do, but our eyes are upon You…" Then the Spirit of the LORD came upon Jahaziel… And he said, "Listen, all you of Judah and you inhabitants of Jerusalem, and you, King Jehoshaphat! Thus says the Lord to you: 'Do not be afraid nor dismayed because of this great multitude, for the battle is not yours, but God's.'"

The king and all the people bow before the Lord, worshiping Him (v. 18). The Levites "stood up to praise the LORD God of Israel with voices loud and high" (v. 19). The next morning as the Israelites march forward, the king cries out (v. 20):

> Hear me, O Judah and you inhabitants of Jerusalem: Believe in the LORD your God, and you shall be established; believe His prophets, and you shall prosper.

Then the king did an amazing thing! He sent the praisers out before the army, and they were singing (v. 21–22):

> "Praise the LORD, for His mercy endures forever." Now when they began to sing and to praise, the LORD set ambushes against the people of Ammon, Moab, and Mount Seir, who had come against Judah; and they were defeated.

The account goes on to say that the enemy began to attack each other, and no one escaped. It took King Jehoshaphat and his people three days to carry away the spoil "because there was so much" (v. 23–25). And in verses 27–28:

> Then they returned, every man of Judah and Jerusalem, with Jehoshaphat in front of them, to go back to Jerusalem with joy, for the Lord had made them rejoice over their enemies. So they came to Jerusalem, with stringed instruments and harps and trumpets, to the house of the Lord.

Is not the "joy of the LORD" our strength (Neh. 8:10); and are we not instructed to put on "the garment of praise for the spirit of heaviness" (Isa. 61:3)? It is difficult to march and fight with a heavy garment.

Paul had wise and potent words for the followers of Christ in Philippians 4:4, when he wrote: "Rejoice in the Lord always. Again I will say, rejoice!" He used the word *rejoice* or *rejoicing* in each of the four chapters (1:26; 2:18; 3:1–2; 4:4); and throughout the letter, he speaks of "joy." I have the following notations written many years ago in my favorite Bible (source unknown): "Joy, gladness. Joy: the emotion excited by the acquisition of expectation of good (Something good is going to happen to you!); gladness: delight, state of happiness, bliss."

In Webster's we find that the prefix "re" means "again" or "back; as before." Paul is showing us that to gain and maintain strength to live victorious lives in Christ we are to "re-joy," over and over and over again, just as we breathe by taking breaths over and over and over again.

This joy is not dependent on circumstances, unlike happiness. Joy is a fruit of the Holy Spirit (Gal. 5:22); and as we yield to the Spirit dwelling within us, the joy comes naturally. Habakkuk, an Old Testament prophet, was experiencing great difficulties, and he wrote:

> Though the fig tree may not blossom, Nor fruit be on the vines; Though the labor of the olive may fail, And the fields yield no food; Though the flock may be cut off from the fold, And there be no herd in the stalls—Yet I will *rejoice* [jump up and down] in the LORD, I will *joy* [be excited, spin around] in the God of my salvation. The LORD God is my *strength*; He will make my feet like deer's feet, And He will make me walk on my high hills.
> —HABAKKUK 3:17–19, EMPHASIS ADDED

Habakkuk made the conscious decision to "rejoice in the Lord" as an act of his will, trusting that His Lord would meet all his needs (Phil. 4:19). We must guard our minds with the helmet of salvation because the enemy will whisper negative words in our ears in an attempt to steal our joy and render us unfruitful in the kingdom. Jesus said in John 15:11:

> These things I have spoken to you, that My joy may remain in you, and that your joy may be full.

Jesus has joy, and He wants us to be full of joy as well. And it is so important to Him that He promises, "Your joy no one will take from you" (John 16:22).

We know that our Father God is a God of joy; just look at our Father's world—bumble bees that fly despite aerodynamics; pansies that look like monkey faces; flower bulbs that look like onions, planted in the dirt in the fall, and in the spring producing glorious blossoms; newborn babies, red and wrinkled, crying and unproductive, yet so beautiful and cherished. The list is endless. (Look in the mirror!) Our Triune God is into this joy thing!

While joy is independent of circumstances, sometimes circumstances can intensify joy, delight, gladness, and bliss. This incident happened to me just yesterday; so I came home and wrote a poem, which I pray will bring a smile to your lips and stir up your joy.

## UNEXPECTED JOY

I was on a routine errand—
Just a quick stop at the Dollar Tree,
When my tickle-box turned over
At a sight that was funny to see.

A woman was struggling with all her might
To hold her gifts in her hands so tight;
They wanted to escape into the air,
But she didn't want them there!

Into her compact car they had to go,
And for an answer she refused to take "No"—
Thirty birthday balloons trying to escape her clutch—
I cannot remember when I laughed so much!

Praise is a vital part of Jewish worship. And David, the prince of worshipers, penned a series of psalms which are called the "Hallel" (Praise of God).

> Hallel (Hebrew, "Praise") is a Jewish prayer—recited verbatim from Psalms 113–118, which is used for praise and thanks giving by observant Jews on Jewish holidays…The first 2 psalms, 113 and 114, are sung before the meal and the remaining 4 after the meal…Psalm 136 which in Jewish liturgy is called "the Great Hallel" [is] recited at the Passover meal after the "Lesser Hallel."[3]

We know that Jesus was a Rabbi, a teacher, and an "observant Jew"; thus it follows that at the Last Supper He and the disciples would have recited Psalms 113 and 114 before the meal, and after the meal had ended, they would have concluded with Psalms 115–118. Our Lord knew that in a matter of hours He would be arrested and the following day He would be crucified, yet He passionately said:

> The stone which the builders rejected [Jesus] Has become the chief cornerstone. This was the Lord's doing; It is marvelous in our eyes. This is the day the Lord has made; We will rejoice and be glad in it.
> —PSALM 118:22–24

The Great Hallel (Ps. 136) is a responsive reading. The priest would recite the first part of the twenty-six verses and the people would respond: "For His mercy endures forever."

God is given thanks and praise for who He is, for creation, and for His deliverance and protection.

The last five psalms of the Book of Psalms, 146–150, are "hallelujah" psalms. Each one begins, "Praise the Lord!" They have the following headings:

- Psalm 146—The Happiness of Those Whose Help Is the Lord;

- Psalm 147—Praise to God for His Word and Providence;

- Psalm 148—Praise to the Lord from Creation;

- Psalm 149—Praise to God for His Salvation and Judgment; and

- Psalm 150—Let All Things Praise the Lord.

In Revelation 19:1–6, we are told by John of a coming "Hallelujah Chorus:"

> After these things I heard a loud voice of a great multitude in heaven, saying, "Alleluia! Salvation and glory and honor and power belong to the Lord our God! For true and righteous are His judgments, because He has judged the great harlot who corrupted the earth with her fornication; and He has avenged on her the blood of His servants shed by her." Again they said, "Alleluia! Her smoke rises up forever and ever!" And the twenty-four elders and the four living creatures fell down and worshiped God who sat on the throne, saying, "Amen! Alleluia!" Then a voice came from the throne, saying, "Praise our God, all you His servants and those who fear Him, both small and great!" And I heard, as it were, the voice of a great multitude, as the sound of many waters and as the sound of mighty

thunderstorms, saying, "Alleluia! For the Lord God Omnipotent reigns!"

Now, singing is not one of my talents; but I can make a joyful noise, and this is one "Hallelujah Chorus" that I do not intend to miss. Come, go with me up that ladder of praise.

## LADDER OF PRAISE

**E. Excellency.** See His excellency! (Isa. 35:2)

**S. Shout.** Shout with the voice of triumph! (Ps. 47:1)

**I. Inspiration.** All scripture is inspired by God. (2 Tim. 3:16)

**A. Access.** We come boldly to His throne of Grace. (Heb. 4:16)

**R. Re-Joice.** His joy is our strength. (Neh. 8:10)

**P. Power of His Presence.** The Lord God Almighty inhabits praise. (Ps. 22:3)

# Chapter 18
# PROMOTION/PARTY TIME

LIFE CAN BE described as the "school of hard knocks." It could also be compared to a pinball machine. God had plans for us before we were born (Eph. 2:10). He put us in exactly the right place, and at exactly the right time (Acts 17:26) we are propelled.

I came into the world on June 13, 1934, as the firstborn of Frank and Elizabeth Terry at Georgia Baptist Hospital in Atlanta, Georgia. I happily rolled along, learning very early that I could get attention by crying loudly. Life was good, even though crying didn't work anymore. And then I hit that first bumper—it was time to go to elementary school. I acquired some social skills and all was well, with the exception of a few (very few) boyfriend bumps. Then I hit a larger bump because I graduated into high school. No longer was I the big fish in the little pond; the pond was like an ocean and I was a shrimp. There was no choice but to roll on; and as I acclimated, I found that I enjoyed learning.

A delightful bump occurred when I was thirteen. At a Sunday school assembly, I asked Jesus to come into my heart. Life was then joyous and I was happily rolling along. The dating thing started, so there were some broken heart bumps, but nothing overwhelming.

Then I hit a really big one when Bob came into my life, and after high school graduation I became his wife. A short time later Bob was drafted and we were stationed in Junction

City, Kansas, where the only job available was secretary to Attorney Weary. This bump was significant because I would need these skills later. Rolling along after discharge, life was beautiful as we added three children to the mix, and there were the usual bumps of their growing up years.

An awesome bump came when I received the fullness of the Holy Spirit, and I rolled along with more meaning and power in my life. I desperately needed this power when three years later I hit a devastating bump; Bob left and I later was divorced. There was no option but to keep rolling and trusting, going through the loss of loved ones, adding new ones, and just the bumps of life in general. My life took a different turn as I earned a double major degree and a subsequent master's.

Doors began to open for missions, bump to go here, another bump to go there, and a bump to teach, write, and speak. Isn't our Lord just something else? He continually guides us along the way; and if we get too far afield, He puts another bump in our path to keep us going in the right direction. As we near the end of our journey, the pathways narrow, and our little ball heads toward home, confident of the promise that the best is yet to be.

We are blessed that this life is an open book test, but I did have a pop quiz just last week. I thought I had finished writing this book and was going back to do some "tweaking." Suddenly the computer screen turned blue and my book was totally gone—zero pages. I know we are to give thanks in all things (1 Thess. 5:18), but I was definitely not thankful. I was sick at my stomach, I was undone, and I was yelling for my daughter upstairs to help me; but she was not home.

I telephoned my computer-wiz friend; she answered and I just screamed, "Help me!" She warned me not to touch anything, promising to call me right back as she had to get out of a computer program she was in at that time. Meanwhile my daughter returned and ran downstairs to rescue me. She kept assuring me that they would get it all back; it was not lost forever. Meanwhile, I tried to stay calm and pray for God's mercy, but it was to no avail. I had definitely lost my peace. It seemed to take forever, but 150 pages were retrieved and I was praising the Lord. All the editing was lost and my last two chapters, but what Satan meant for evil, God worked into another testimony of His grace.

Hindsight is 20/20. We can look back and see God's hand, but looking ahead is not quite that easy. We must "walk by faith, not by sight" (2 Cor. 5:7). Many times we hit those bumps, "but God." Notice how many times in the Bible we can read an account of impending tragedy, and then there are those two little words, "but God," and things turn around. The hero or "she-ro" comes out conquering and victorious.

Abraham was called by God to be the father of nations, but he went through that bumpy time with Hagar. Jacob, the deceiver, reaped deceit but he became the father of the twelve tribes. Joseph's dream of power and authority did not materialize until he had endured the pit and the prison. David was anointed king of Israel, but he was not crowned until he passed through the cave days. Mary's promise of her son being the Messiah was not as she had planned, for a sword did pierce her soul also (Luke 2:35), and she experienced the crucifixion before the resurrection.

England was facing its darkest hour in the fall of 1941 before America entered World War II. Winston Churchill, the prime minister, gave the following speech to the boys at Harrow School:

> Never, never—in nothing, great or small, large or petty—never give in except to convictions of honour and good sense. Never yield to force; never yield to the apparently overwhelming might of the enemy.[1]

The only time we lose is when we quit. Jesus promised that if we just have "faith as a grain of mustard seed...nothing will be impossible for you" (Matt. 17:20).

The Holy Spirit is hard at work in our lives, transforming us into the image of Jesus, and moving us from glory to glory (2 Cor. 3:18). The glory part sounds wonderful, but in between each mountaintop is a valley, and that is where we do the most growing. But we are not to despair, for Jesus said to "cheer up!" We are overcomers (John 16:33).

Many years ago the Lord asked me a question: "When in your life have things not worked out for you?" Duh! Never! When I am struggling with an issue and trying to get a "word from the Lord," often He will answer me by asking that same question, and I have to laugh (at myself). I regret that I am such a slow learner.

Another trap of the enemy that is easy to fall into is that of comparing ourselves to others. Each one of God's children is unique—one of a kind; and each one fits into God's master plan. Our talents vary, but when we put them all together, we are building a kingdom. A young lad with a lunch was used by Jesus to feed more than five thousand people, and all he had to do was give Jesus what he had (John 6:1–14). I bet his mother packed that lunch. Jesus told the disciples to gather up the leftovers, "so that nothing is lost" (v. 12). We see two things here: first, there is a network (we are all needed to cover our world for Christ); and secondly, there are no small things in God's kingdom. I repeat: He does not waste anything.

I heard a story of a mission trip to Peru, where a minister was to preach at a certain village located by a river. As they were traveling upstream in a canoe, the current was so strong against them that they seemed to be making no headway. He became very frustrated, crying out to the Lord that he had not come to Peru just to sit in a canoe. The Lord replied, "If you cannot serve Me in this canoe, I do not need you speaking in a pulpit."

Whatever task is set before us each day is the most important task, whether it is speaking from a pulpit or rowing a canoe. When we diligently perform that task to the best of our ability, we are set up for promotion. Jesus said, "He who is faithful in what is least is also faithful in much" (Luke 16:10).

We can be encouraged with God's promise as contained in Psalm 37: (This is so good!)

> Don't be impatient for the Lord to act! Keep traveling steadily along his pathway and in due season he will honor you with every blessing…For the good man—the blameless, the upright, the man of peace—he has a wonderful future ahead of him. For him there is a happy ending.
>
> —PSALM 37:34, 37, TLB

Don't you love happy endings—especially when they are yours? Speaking of happy endings, let's go back and join that Hallelujah Chorus that was singing in Revelation 19:1–6.

> "Let us be glad and rejoice and give Him glory, for the marriage of the Lamb has come and His wife has made herself ready." And to her it was granted to be arrayed in fine linen, clean and bright, for the fine linen is the righteousness of the saints. Then he said

to me, "Write: 'Blessed are those who are called to the marriage supper of the Lamb.'" And he said to me, "These are the true sayings of God."

—REVELATION 19:7–9

The followers of Christ have long been rehearsing for the marriage supper of the Lamb by partaking of Holy Communion, celebrating His passion for us through the sacrifice of His body and His blood on the cross of Calvary in payment of the ransom for our sin. Now the waiting is over, our work is done, the last name has been recorded, and the books are closed. The Father reaches over, taps His Son on the shoulder, and says, "Go! Bring my children home." It's party time!

# THE PARTY

Are you going to the party?
Everybody who's anybody will be there!

There will be joy and laughter—no tears or woes,
And we will all be dressed in the finest of robes—
Pure white, without spot or blemish, I'm told,

And wine will be served in goblets of gold.
The food will be sumptuous—fit for a king.
The music will be heavenly; we'll hear angels sing.
There will be plenty of time to visit and talk,
And after dinner, you and Jesus can walk.

Of course, this affair is by invitation only,
Purchased by our Lord at the Cross of Calvary.
It will be a time to honor the Christ, God's Son,
And praise Him for His work on earth, so well done.

Be sure and tell everybody you're able—
There's plenty of room at our Lord's table.
He doesn't want anyone to stay away,
He went to great expense to pay our way.

I certainly hope to see you in your reserved place,
For I shall be there—by God's Amazing Grace!

# CONCLUSION

**D**EAR READER, I am finding it hard to say goodbye to you. That's the way it is when you are enjoying the pleasure of someone's company over a meal. It has brought me much joy to share "taters and peas" with you, and I thank you for graciously accepting my invitation to dine.

We began on the premise of a children's sermonette and expanded from there, hopefully with some "meaty" parts for you to chew on. We have ended with an invitation to the party of all parties—the marriage supper of the Lamb. Just the anticipation brings a smile, but it is imperative that you make your reservation in advance, before the Book of Life is closed.

Jesus said to come like little children and it is as easy as A-B-C. Just admit that you are a sinner, believe in the finished work of Jesus on the cross, and commit your life to Him. You invite Him into your heart as Lord and Savior, and He invites you into His Kingdom—and to the party! The Holy Spirit will be your Helper and Guide.

I'll see you there, and please bring with you as many as you can, because the more the merrier!

# NOTES

### CHAPTER 2
### COMMENT-TATER

1.   "Walter Cronkite," *Wikipedia*, last modified April 12, 2014, http://en.wikipedia.org/wiki/Walter_Cronkite (accessed April 20, 2014).

2.   "Thomas the Apostle," *Wikipedia*, last modified April 19, 2014, http://en.wikipedia.org/wiki/Thomas_the_Apostle (accessed April 20, 2013).

### CHAPTER 3
### SPEC-TATER

1.   Betty Smith, *Around the World in Seventy Years* (Lake Mary, FL: Creation House, 2008).

2.   "Robert Browning Quotes," *Goodreads Inc.*, http://www.goodreads.com/author/quotes/24391.Robert_Browning (accessed April 21, 2014).

### CHAPTER 4
### PARTICIPA-TATER

1.   "Just Do It," *Wikipedia*, last modified March 24, 2014, http://en.wikipedia.org/wiki/Just_Do_It (accessed April 21, 2014).

### CHAPTER 5
### GIFTS

1.   W. E. Vine, *Vine's Expository Dictionary of New Testament Words*, (McLean, VA: McDonald Publishing, 1985), 703.

2.   "Quotes for Han Solo (character) from *Star Wars* (1977)," *IMBd.com, Inc.*, http://www.imdb.com/character/ch0000002/quotes (accessed April 21, 2014).

### CHAPTER 7
### CROWNS

1.   "Betty Davis Quotes," *Goodreads Inc.*, http://www.goodreads.com/author/quotes/56410.Bette_Davis-42k (accessed April 21, 2014).

## Chapter 8
### Irri-Tater

1.  Jean Paul Richter, Today Books, *Today.com*, http://www.today.com/id/4693847/hs/today_today_books/t/putting_your__trust_in_god (accessed April 22, 2014).
2.  "Edmund Burke," *Wikiquote.org*, http://en/wikiquote.org.wiki/Edmund_Burke last modified April 12, 2014, (accessed April 22, 2014).
3.  "John Wesley," *Goodreads Inc.*, http://www.goodreads.com/author/quotes/151350.John Wesley (accessed April 22, 2014).
4.  Henry Halley, *Halley's Bible Handbook* (Grand Rapids, MI: Zondervan, 1962), 239.
5.  Sarah Young, *Jesus Calling* (Nashville, TN: Thomas Nelson, 2004), 215.

## Chapter 9
### Imi-Tater

1.  "Charles Caleb Colton Quotes," *BrainyQuote*, http://www.brainyquote.com/quotes/authors/c/charles_caleb_colton.html (April 22, 2014).

## Chapter 10
### Sweet Tater

1.  Porter L. Barrington, *The Christian Life Bible* (Nashville, TN: Thomas Nelson, 1985).

## Chapter 12
### God's Peas

1.  "Goober Peas," *Wikipedia*, last modified September 13, 2013, http://en.wikipedia.org/wiki/Goober_Peas (April 22, 2014).

## Chapter 13
### Promises

1.  Laurence Urdang, *The American Century Dictionary* (New York: Warner Books, 1996), 461.
2.  Ibid., s.v. "promise."
3.  Ibid., s.v. "Promised Land."
4.  "Happy 65th, Dear Israel," Morim Madrichim Newsletter 82 (April 2013) http://www.jewishprograms.org/nwltool/nwl_files/996/html/view.aspx (accessed April 23, 2014).

5.    John Hagee, *Jerusalem Countdown* (Lake Mary, FL: Front-line, 2006), 45.

CHAPTER 14
PRAYER

1.    "The Umbilical Cord," Family Education, *Pearson Education, Inc.*, http://pregnancy.familyeducation.com/prenatal-health-and-nutrition/fetal-growth-and-development/66161.html (accessed April 24, 2014).

2.    "Charlotte Cushman Quotes," *LifeQuotesLib.com*, http://www.lifequoteslib.com/authors/charlotte_cushman.html (accessed April 22, 2014).

3.    Dr. Charles Stanley, "Praying On the Armor of God," April 28–29, 2007, InTouch Ministries http://www.intouch.org/magazine/content/topic/4433#.U1Z3pVVdVSs (accessed April 22, 2014).

4.    "There's a Light Shining Forth," SmallChurchMusic.com, www.smallchurchmusic3com/Lyrics/D03/S03568.php (accessed April 29, 2014).

CHAPTER 15
PROTECTION

1.    Saint John of the Cross, translated by A.Z. Foreman, "The Dark Night of the Soul," "Saint John of the Cross: The Dark Night of the Soul (From Spanish),"*Poems Found in Translation* (blog), http://poemsintranslation.blogspot.com/2009/09/saint-john-of-cross-dark-night-of-soul.html (accessed April 24, 2014).

2.    "Dark Night of the Soul," *Wikipedia*, last modified February 13, 2013, *http://en.wikipedia.org/wiki/Dark_Night_of_the_Soul* (accessed April 24, 2014).

3.    Barrington.

4.    Dutch Sheets, *Intercessory Prayer* (Ventura, CA: Regal Books, 1996), 43.

5.    Ibid., 44–45.

CHAPTER 16
PERSEVERANCE

1.    Denny, "A Diamond Is Merely a Lump of Coal That Did Well Under the Pressure," *Look up at the Sky for Inspiration* (blog), February 14, 2011, http://lookupatthesky.wordpress.

com/2011/02/14/a-diamond-is-merely-a-lump-of-coal-that-did-well-under-the-pressure/ (accessed April 22, 2014).

## CHAPTER 17
### PRAISE

1.  Merlin Carothers, *Prison to Praise* (Escondido, CA: Foundation of Praise, 1970), 90, 98–99.
2.  Ibid.
3.  "Hallel," *Wikipedia*, last modified April 14, 2013, http://en.wikipedia.org/wiki/Hallel (accessed April 23, 2014).

## CHAPTER 18
### PROMOTION/PARTY TIME

1.  Winston Churchill, "Never Given In," speech given at Harrow School on October 29, 2011, *The Churchill Centre*, http://www.winstonchurchill.org/learn/speeches/speeches-of-winston-churchill/103-never-give-in (accessed April 23, 2014).

# ABOUT THE AUTHOR

**B**ETTY T. SMITH is a native Georgian and a retired legal secretary. She has a master's degree in Christian counseling from Logos Christian College in Jacksonville, Florida. She currently worships with her family at Powder Springs United Methodist Church, where she teaches an adult Sunday school class and a women's Bible study; she also serves on the Prayer Force and Visitation Team. She is a volunteer prayer counselor at Family Life Ministries, a ministry to the homeless, poor, and those in financial and emotional distress.

In 2008 Betty published her first book, *Around the World in Seventy Years*, which covers sixteen mission trips to places as close as Mexico and New York City and as far away as China and Siberia. Her second book, *Nothing Wasted*, is the story of God's faithfulness and integrity as He keeps His promise of restoration. Her third book, *Beyond the Happy Ending*, shows how God not only keeps His promises but takes you exceedingly and abundantly *beyond*.

Betty is the mother of two sons and one daughter and the grandmother of five; she considers this to be her greatest legacy.

# CONTACT THE AUTHOR

Website:
www.bettyterrysmith.com

E-mail:
betty@bettyterrysmith.com

# MORE BOOKS
## TO EDIFY & INSPIRE YOU

CREATION HOUSE HAS BEEN AN INDUSTRY LEADER FOR
MORE THAN 40 YEARS WITH WORLDWIDE DISTRIBUTION AND
A REPUTATION FOR QUALITY AND INTEGRITY.

WAYNE ABEL

978-1-62136-387-3
$10.99 US

AMY SANDERS

978-1-62136-392-7
$16.99 US

RANDALL JAMES

978-1-62136-396-5
$16.99 US

STEVE RICHARD

978-1-62136-672-0
$14.99 US

# VISIT YOUR LOCAL BOOKSTORE
## WWW.CREATIONHOUSE.COM

## RETAILERS: CALL 1-800-283-8494
### WWW.CHARISMAHOUSEB2B.COM

## CREATION
## HOUSE

12461